VIEWER'S GUIDE 1

EPISODES 1–13

HOWARD BECKERMAN

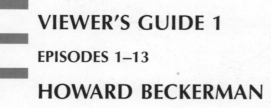

Family Album, U.S.A.

Teleplays by Alvin Cooperman and George Lefferts

MAXWELL MACMILLAN ◀

INTERNATIONAL PUBLISHING GROUP ◀

New York   Oxford   Singapore   Sydney

COLLIER MACMILLAN CANADA ◀

Toronto

Collier Macmillan Canada
1200 Eglinton Avenue E.
Don Mills, Ontario M3C 3N1

Director: *Karen Peratt*
Executive Editor: *Mary Jane Peluso*
Development Editor: *Allene Feldman*
Assistant Editor: *Agatha Lorenzo*

Cover Design: *BB&K*
Illustrations: *Shelley Matheis*
Interior Design: *BB&K; Publication Services, Inc.*
Production Services: *Publication Services, Inc.*
Production Coordinator: *Marcia Craig*

Photo credits: All photos by Eric Liebowitz, except for the following: Courtesy of Howard Beckerman: **18** (top). Courtesy of Bill Higgins: **22** (top). Courtesy of Jim Sulley: **40** (bottom), **70** (top). Courtesy of Roberto Pires: **66**. Special thanks to the Sony Corporation for permission to use photo of Walkman personal stereo ®, a registered trademark: **74** (top). Courtesy of University of Michigan: **101** (bottom). Special thanks to The Dovetail Group, Inc., Cynthia Vansant, photographer, for all screen lifts from video.

This book was set in Optima
and printed and bound by Maxwell Macmillan Publishing Singapore Pte Ltd
The cover was printed by Maxwell Macmillan Publishing Singapore Pte Ltd

Printing: 3 4 5 6 7   Year: 0 1 2 3 4 5 6

Maxwell Macmillan International Publishing Group
ESL/EFL Department, 866 Third Avenue, New York, NY 10022

Printed in Singapore

ISBN 0–02–332771–5

Contents

Acknowledgments

The long and winding road . . .

This is the phrase that comes to mind whenever I think of ELTB. ELTB has been a long and winding road full of dedication, errors, learning, disappointment, amazement, and now, elation. The first materials are going public . . .

There have been many people who have helped us get down this road and many more who have cheered from the sidelines. I am certain that the following acknowledgments do not include everyone who has made a special contribution—I have forgotten someone. With apologies for the inevitable oversight, I would like to thank the following people:

For the early vision and risks, Robert Baensch and the late Lois Roth; for keeping us safe and continuing to believe, Jack Farnsworth; for overcoming disbelief and for always being there, Mary Jane Peluso; for dedication and day-to-day-to-day hard work, Allene Feldman; for creativity, talent, and inspiration, Howard Beckerman; for unswerving guidance, Diane Larsen-Freeman; and for understanding and support, all the members of the ESL/EFL Department: Maggie Barbieri, Gloria Cazón de Pascual, Debbie Devine, Aggie Lorenzo, Betty Mirando, and Kelly Ramsey.

Robert Curran, Stuart Leigh, and Frank Beardsley produced a superb radio series, *Tuning In the U.S.A.* Alvin Cooperman pulled together a great television team for *Family Album, U.S.A.* and beat the odds on costs. The Dovetail Group—Gerri Brioso, Richard Freitas, Paul Freitas, and Cynthia Vansant—made the "Focus In" segments joys to behold. Tina Peel and Greg Orr are not to be forgotten for their contribution in the rough early days.

The ELTB Advisory Board provided much support and guidance during a very long period, and they deserve many thanks: Russell Campbell, chairman, Lyle Bachman, William Greaves, Diane Larsen-Freeman, Marc Pachter, and Chiz Schultz.

The educators, broadcasters, and publishers from around the world who provided us with invaluable insight and resources are too numerous to name.

And finally, a special thank you to all the people who helped us get ELTB off the ground. I trust that we will not have disappointed you with the fruits of our efforts.

Karen Peratt
Project Director

Introduction

Welcome to *Family Album, U.S.A.*, the exciting new American television series created to inspire English learning around the world. In 26 episodes, you will experience English in action and learn more about American culture. *Family Album, U.S.A.* is for everyone who has studied English for at least one year and wants to improve his or her understanding of the language.

Each television episode tells a story about the Stewarts, a typical American family living in New York. You will see the family in everyday situations, and you will share their many experiences as you hear English spoken naturally.

The unique format of each television program includes the following:

PREVIEW
Before each of the three acts in an episode, a story preview sets the scene and introduces important vocabulary to aid comprehension. The preview usually asks a question for you to think about as you watch the act. Words on the screen help prepare you for the upcoming drama.

DRAMA
Each episode tells a complete story. In every drama, you follow the lives of the Stewart family at work or at play. Each episode centers around one important event, such as a holiday celebration, a job interview, a wedding, or the birth of a baby. The language level in the dramas follows a sequence. Grammar and vocabulary are simpler in the earlier episodes. In the later episodes, the language is more advanced.

FOCUS IN
After each act, a lively "Focus In" segment calls your attention to idioms, grammar, pronunciation, useful expressions, story comprehension, or important information about life in the U.S. The "Focus In" segments entertain you with music, animation, and humor as they highlight language and culture.

This *Viewer's Guide* will help you understand Episodes 1–13 of the series. On these pages, you will find a unique way to study the television programs. Each lesson follows this easy format:

PREVIEW PAGE
Before each episode, a preview page prepares you for the story as well as for the language points in the episode. On this page, three key photographs introduce you to the three acts of the drama. A summary of important language and cultural points previews the material that you will study in the *Viewer's Guide* episode.

SCRIPT AND LANGUAGE NOTES   The complete script for each drama follows the preview page. The script always appears in the left column of a page. Beside the script, colorful photographs, artwork, and many language notes are provided to help you understand the drama. In addition, facts about U.S. life are introduced. A "Your Turn" feature asks you to compare your own culture with aspects of American life.

ACTIVITIES PAGE   A page of language and comprehension activities follows the script for each act. The first activity always relates to the "Focus In" segment. Additional activities give you a chance to practice language skills.

ANSWER KEY   An Answer Key at the back of the book lets you check your answers to the exercises on the three Activities pages in each episode.

USEFUL VOCABULARY AND EXPRESSIONS   The *Viewer's Guide* ends with an alphabetical list of all words and expressions that appear in the language notes beside the scripts. Next to each item, the episode number appears in parentheses for easy reference.

You can study an episode in the *Viewer's Guide* before *or* after you watch the program. It's up to you.

Family Album, U.S.A. is designed to be entertaining and educational in an easy-to-follow format. We hope that this *Viewer's Guide* will be your companion to enjoying and understanding this innovative television series.

THE CHARACTERS

Here are the people you will meet in *Family Album, U.S.A.*

MALCOLM STEWART   also known as Grandpa, 72, a retired engineer who comes to live with his son and his son's family in Riverdale, New York

PHILIP STEWART   Malcolm's son, 50, a doctor

ELLEN STEWART   Philip's wife, 50, a homemaker and a former music teacher

RICHARD STEWART   Philip and Ellen's older son, 30, a photographer

MARILYN STEWART   Richard's wife, 29, a salesclerk in a boutique and a clothing designer

ROBBIE STEWART   Philip and Ellen's younger son, 17, a senior in high school

SUSAN STEWART   Philip and Ellen's daughter, 28, a vice-president of a toy company, unmarried and living in an apartment in Manhattan

HARRY BENNETT   an accountant, 33, a widower who dates Susan

MICHELLE BENNETT   Harry's daughter, 9

MOLLY BAKER   a nurse, 43, who works with Philip in the hospital

ALEXANDRA PAPPAS   an exchange student from Greece, 16, Robbie's friend

. . . and other friends and business associates

Language and Culture Sequence

"46 Linden Street"

ACT I

ACT II

ACT III

In this episode, you will study . . .

[épisoud]

VOCABULARY [və'kæbjuləri]

photographer   boutique
exchange student   dessert
toy   pediatrician

GRAMMAR AND EXPRESSIONS

introducing yourself [introdjues]
responding to introductions
introducing others
asking for permission
thanking
accepting thanks
the order of adjectives [edjikkive]

PRONUNCIATION [prənaunsiéɪʃən]

I've got to . . . (I've gotta)
Let me . . . (Lemme)
hour (Hour)

U.S. LIFE

• What is the population of the United States?
• What is special about the subway system in New York City?

☞ YOUR TURN

• From which nations do immigrants come to your country?
• How do most people travel to work in your city or town?

Here is the complete script with study material for Episode 1. Use these materials before *or* after you watch.

ACT I

On a ferryboat in New York Harbor. We can see the Statue of Liberty. Richard Stewart, 30, is taking pictures.

Richard: **Excuse me.**[1] **My name is** [2] Richard Stewart. I'm a **photographer.**[3] May I[4] take a picture of you and your little boy?

Mrs. Vann: What's it for?

Richard: It's for a book.

Mrs. Vann: You're writing a book?

Richard: It's a book of **pictures.**[5] I call it *Family Album, U.S.A.*

Mrs. Vann: Oh, that's a nice idea. Well, it's fine if you take our picture. I'm Martha Vann. *[She offers her hand.]*

Richard: Thank you. **I appreciate your help.**[6] *[to the little boy]* **I'm**[7] Richard. What's your name?

Gerald: Gerald.

Richard: How old are you, Gerald?

Gerald: Five.

Richard: And where do you live?

Mrs. Vann: We live in **California.**[8]

Richard: Well, welcome to New York. OK, just a second. *[He takes out a reflector to have more light for his photographs.]* I'm almost ready here.

[Alexandra, a sixteen-year-old girl, is watching.]

Alexandra: Can I help you?

Richard: Oh, please. *[He gives her the reflector to hold. Then he speaks to Mrs. Vann and her son.]* Hold Gerald's hand, please. Great! Now **point**[9] to the buildings. Terrific! Give Mommy a kiss, Gerald. Nice! Thank you, Gerald. And thank you, Mrs. Vann.

Statue of Liberty

[1] Excuse me.
Use this expression to get someone's attention.

[2] My name is . . .
Use this phrase to introduce yourself.

[3] photographer
A photographer's job is to take pictures with a camera.

[4] May I . . . ? = Can I . . . ?
Use *May I* or *Can I* to ask for permission. *May* is more polite than *can.*

[5] pictures: photographs

[6] I appreciate your help. = Thank you for helping me.

[7] I'm . . .
Use *I'm* to introduce yourself.

[8] California

[9] point: to use your finger to show direction

Mrs. Vann: Oh, **my pleasure.**[10] We'll be looking for your book.

Richard: Thank you. Good-bye. **Bye,**[11] Gerald. *[to Alexandra]* **Thanks**[12] again.

Alexandra: Oh, **you're welcome.**[13]

Richard: **Hey,**[14] let me take your picture!

Alexandra: Wonderful. Please.

Richard: Are you from New York?

Alexandra: No, I'm from **Greece.**[15] I'm an **exchange student.**[16]

Richard: When did you come here?

Alexandra: Three months ago.

Richard: Your English is very good.

Alexandra: Thanks. I studied English in school.

[They sit on a bench.]

Richard: Would you like some coffee?

Alexandra: No, thank you. Tell me about your book.

Richard: Oh, it's not finished yet, but I have some of the pictures. Would you like to see them?

Alexandra: Yes. I'd like that.

Richard: **Here they are.**[17] *[He opens his bag and takes out a **photo album.**[18]] Family Album, U.S.A.* It's an album of pictures of the United States: the cities, the special places, and the people. *[He shows her the photos.]* And these are pictures of people working: steelworkers, bankers, police, street vendors, ambulance drivers, doctors. . . . Oh, this is my father. He's a doctor. This is my mother.

"It's an album of pictures of the United States."

[10] **My pleasure.**
Use this expression after someone says *Thank you.*

[11] **Bye.** = Good-bye.

[12] **Thanks.** = Thank you

[13] **You're welcome.**
Use this expression after someone says *Thank you.*

[14] **Hey!**
This word shows that Richard has a new idea. It is a very informal word.

[15] **Greece**

[16] **exchange student**
An *exchange student* goes to school in a different country for a short time and lives with a family in that country.

[17] **Here they are.** = They are here.
This word order is common when you find something and want to show it.

[18] **photo album:** a book of photographs

steelworker

ambulance driver   **street vendor**

Alexandra: What's her name?

Richard: Ellen. My younger brother, Robbie. He goes to high school. This is my sister Susan. She works for a **toy**[19] company. Here's my grandfather. He lives in Florida. And this is my wife Marilyn.

Alexandra: Oh, she's very pretty.

Richard: Thanks. And **what about**[20] your family?

Alexandra: They are in Thessaloniki. That's a large city in northern Greece. But now I'm living in **the Bronx.**[21]

Richard: With a Greek-American family?

Alexandra: No. **Hispanic.**[22]

Richard: [He hears a foghorn.] Oh no! It's **five thirty.**[23] Will you excuse me? I have to meet my wife.

Alexandra: **It was nice meeting you.**[24]

Richard: **It was a pleasure meeting you,**[25] too. Thanks for your help. And good luck! **I've got to go.**[26] **By the way,**[27] I'm Richard. What's your name?

Alexandra: Alexandra.

Richard: Bye-bye, Alexandra. Thanks.

Alexandra: Bye-bye. [Richard hurries off the boat. Alexandra sees that he forgot one of his bags. She takes it and begins to follow him.] Richard! Richard! You left your bag!

END OF ACT I

Dr. Phillip Stewart

Ellen Stewart

Robbie Stewart and Susan Stewart

Grandpa Malcolm Stewart and Marilyn Stewart

[19] **toy:** something a child plays with

[20] **What about . . . ?** = Tell me about . . . [보아라]

[21] **the Bronx:** one of the five boroughs, or areas, of New York City. The other boroughs are Manhattan, Brooklyn, Queens, and Staten Island. [ailand]

[22] **Hispanic:** Spanish-speaking

[23] **five thirty:**

[24] **It was nice meeting you.** = [25] **It was a pleasure meeting you.**

Use these expressions to say good-bye after meeting someon for the first time.

[26] **I've got to go.** = I must go.
The informal pronunciation is *I've gotta go.*

[27] **By the way . . .**
Use this phrase to change the topic of conversation.

🏳 U.S. LIFE

The population of the United States is over 250 million people, including more than 22 million Hispanics. Alexandra is living with an Hispanic family while she studies in New York City.

☞ YOUR TURN

• Do many foreigners live in your country?
• From which nations do these foreigners, or immigrants, come?

ACT I *Activities*

Here are some activities to help you check your understanding of Act I.

FAMILY ALBUM, U.S.A.

What did Alexandra learn about Richard and his family? What did Richard learn about Alexandra? Read the facts in the box. Then write each fact on the line under the correct picture. The first answer is given.

Her name is Ellen.	She's Richard's wife.	He's a doctor.	He's a photographer.
He goes to high school.	She works for a toy company.	She's from Greece.	He lives in Florida.

1.

He's a photographer.

2.

She's from greece

3.

She work for a toy company

4.

She's Richard's wife.

5.

He goes to high school

6.

Her name is Ellen

7.
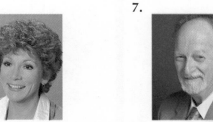
He lives in florida

8.

He's a doctor

STORY LINES

What is the correct order of the following events in Act I? Write the number *1, 2, 3, 4,* or *5* on each line to show the correct sequence. The first answer is given.

2 **a.** Richard photographs Alexandra.
5 **b.** Richard leaves his bag on the boat.
4 **c.** Richard tells Alexandra his name.
1 **d.** Alexandra offers to help Richard.
3 **e.** Richard shows Alexandra some photos.

ACT II

Outside the ferry building. Alexandra sees Richard leave in a taxicab. She asks a policeman for directions.

Alexandra: Excuse me, officer. Can you help me?

Policeman: Sure.

Alexandra: Can you tell me how to get to Linden Street, in Riverdale?

Policeman: [He reads the name tag on Richard's bag.] "Richard Stewart, 46 Linden Street, Riverdale, New York." You should take the number 1 subway.

Alexandra: Is there a station near here?

Policeman: Yes. The station's that way. You should take the number 1 train to Van Cortlandt Park.

Alexandra: Number 1 train to Van Cortlandt Park. Thank you.

Policeman: **Anytime.**[1] Good luck. Remember, the number 1 train. The **uptown platform.**[2]

Alexandra: Thank you.

Policeman: You're welcome.

[Alexandra walks toward the subway entrance. She passes the "uptown" sign.]

In a boutique.[3] **Marilyn Stewart, Richard's wife, is helping a customer.**

Customer: Is this pink too bright for me?

Marilyn: Mmm-hmm. It is a very bright pink. Try this. *[She takes a red sweater from a table.]* It's size eight.

Customer: But I wear size ten.

Marilyn: How about green? It's size ten.

Customer: **Let me**[4] **try it on.**[5]

[Marilyn looks at her watch.]

Customer: I'm taking too much of your time.

Marilyn: It's **six o'clock.**[6] Where's my husband? I was expecting him here at **five forty-five.**[7]

[1] **Anytime.** = My pleasure.
Use *Anytime* after someone thanks you for doing something.

[2] **uptown platform:** the place to wait for trains going north

[3] **boutique:** a small store that sells clothing and other special items

[4] **Let me . . .** = Permit me . . .
The customer uses an informal pronunciation. She says *Lemme.*

[5] **try (it) on**
You *try on* an item of clothing to be sure that the size is correct and that you like the way it looks.

[6] **six o'clock:**

[7] **five forty-five:**

U.S. LIFE

Alexandra is taking the subway to Richard's house. The New York City subway system is the longest underground train system in the world. The subway runs 137 miles (220.6 kilometers) under the city.

☞ YOUR TURN

- How do most people travel to work in your city or town?

- Is there a subway system in your country?

Customer: Don't worry. **The traffic is very heavy**[8] at this **hour.**[9]

Marilyn: I know. But we're going to be late for dinner.

Customer: I'll take this green sweater. I like the color on me, don't you?

Marilyn: I think it looks terrific on you.

A little later. Richard rushes into the boutique.

Richard: I'm sorry I'm so late. I had a really bad day.

Marilyn: It's **ten after six.**[10] We're late. Robbie's cooking tonight, and dinner's at **six thirty.**[11]

Richard: I know. I know. I'm really sorry. I left my bag of film on the ferry. I went back for it, but the ferry was gone. I lost a whole day's work.

Marilyn: I'll call the Staten Island Ferry **lost-and-found office.**[12]

Richard: I didn't think of that. Thanks.

Marilyn: *[She picks up the telephone and dials the number for information.]* Hello. Yes. The number, please, of the Staten Island Ferry lost-and-found office. Five five five...zero eight zero eight. Thank you. *[She hangs up and dials the number.]*

Richard: I really appreciate it, Marilyn.

Marilyn: Hello. Did anyone find a camera bag this afternoon, a **small canvas bag,**[13] on the J. F. Kennedy Ferry?...No? Maybe someone *will* find it. The name is Stewart, Richard Stewart. And the telephone number is five five five...three oh nine oh. Thank you. *[She hangs up.]* Sorry, Richard. They don't have it.

Richard: **Thanks, anyway.**[14] *[thinking]* There was a girl on the ferry. Now maybe . . .

Marilyn: Tell me about it on the way home.

END OF ACT II

[hevi]

[8] **The traffic is very heavy.** = There are many cars.

[9] **hour**
Do not pronounce the letter *h* in this word. *Hour* sounds the same as the word *our*.

[10] **ten after six:**

[11] **six thirty:**

[12] **lost-and-found office**
If you find something that doesn't belong to you, you can take it to a *lost-and-found* office. People can go to this office to get their lost things.

[13] **small canvas bag:**
Two adjectives describe the bag: *Small* tells the size; *canvas* tells the material. The order of adjectives is size before material.

"a small canvas bag"

[14] **Thanks, anyway.**
Use this expression to thank someone who tries to help but isn't able to.

帆布 [kæn vəs]

New York City

ACT II

Activities

Here are some activities to help you check your understanding of Act II.

"THANK YOU"
"YOU'RE WELCOME"

These are some ways to say *Thank You* and *You're welcome*.

Use these expressions to thank someone:	Use these expressions <u>after</u> someone says *Thank you*:
Thank you.	**You're welcome.**
Thank you very much.	**I'm glad that I could help.**
It was very nice of you.	**Glad that I could help.**
I appreciate your help.	**Don't mention it.**
I appreciate it.	**It was nothing.**
Use this expression to thank someone who tries to help but isn't able to:	**My pleasure.**
	Anytime.
Thanks, anyway.	

Complete each of the following lines by choosing *a* or *b*. Circle the letter of each corect answer.

1. Richard: (*to Mrs. Vann*) Thank you. *I appreciate your help*.
   a. I appreciate your help   **b**. My pleasure

2. Richard: Thank you, Gerald. And thank you, Mrs. Vann.
   Mrs. Vann: Oh, *my pleasure*.
   a. I appreciate your help   **b**. my pleasure

3. Alexandra: (*to the policeman*): Number 1 train to Van Cortlandt Park. Thank you.
   Policeman: _____*Anytime*_____. Good luck.
   a. It was very nice of you   **b**. Anytime

4. Marilyn: (*on the telephone to the lost-and-found office*) Thank you.
   (*to Richard*) Sorry, Richard. They don't have it.
   Richard: *thanks anyway*.
   a. Thanks, anyway   **b**. Don't mention it

FIND THE NUMBERS

Draw a line from each question at the left to the correct number or time at the right. The first one is done for you. You may need to reread the script for Act II to find the answers. Try to complete this activity in less than two minutes!

1. What is the number of Richard's house on Linden Street?   **a**. 555-0808
2. Which train does Alexandra need to take?   **b**. 46
3. Which size does Marilyn's customer wear?   **c**. 6:30
4. What time did Marilyn expect Richard to arrive at the boutique?   **d**. 10
5. What time is Robbie going to serve dinner?   **e**. 555-3090
6. What is Richard's home telephone number?   **f**. 5:45
7. What is the telephone number of the lost-and-found office?   **g**. 1

ACT III

At the Stewarts' home in Riverdale that evening. Philip is on the phone with one of his patients.

Philip: And give her a teaspoon of the medicine after every meal. Don't worry. She'll be fine. You're welcome. Good-bye.

Ellen: *[She enters.]* How are you?

Philip: I'm tired and hungry.

Ellen: Well, Marilyn and Richard called. They'll be here soon, and then we'll eat.

Philip: All right. Is . . . is Susan coming?

Ellen: Well, she'll be here later. She has to work late tonight.

Philip: And what's Robbie cooking for dinner?

Ellen: It's a surprise.

Philip: I hope it's **pasta.**[1]

Later that evening. Philip, Ellen, Richard, Marilyn, Susan, and Robbie are in the Stewarts' kitchen.

Philip: Robbie, the dinner was terrific.

Susan: Yes, it was delicious.

Marilyn: What's for **dessert?**[2]

Robbie: Oh, I forgot dessert.

Philip: Robbie!

Ellen: Don't worry. **We've got**[3] lots of ice cream. *[She goes to the refrigerator.]*

Richard: Oh, I'd love some ice cream.

Ellen: Well, there's chocolate and coffee and a little vanilla.

Robbie: I'll have vanilla. Is that all right with everyone?

Philip: I'll have chocolate.

Marilyn: **Me, too.**[4]

Richard: Uh, one **scoop**[5] of coffee and one scoop of chocolate for me.

Ellen: Robbie, will you help me serve?

[Robbie gets up to help. Richard brings the ice-cream dishes to Ellen.]

Richard: I keep thinking about that bag of film. Eight rolls. A whole day's work. And good **stuff,**[6] too.

Ellen: Don't worry, Richard. Someone will find it.

[The doorbell rings.]

[1] **pasta:**

[2] **dessert:** something sweet at the end of a meal

[3] **We've got** . . . = We have got . . .
The meaning is the same as "We have."

[4] **Me, too.** = I'll also have chocolate ice cream.

[5] **scoop:**

[6] **stuff:** things
Here, Richard is referring to his photographs.

Robbie:	I'll get it. *[He opens the door. Alexandra is standing there. She is holding Richard's bag of film.]* Hello.
Alexandra:	Hello. Does Richard Stewart live here?
Robbie:	Yes, he's my brother. I'm Robbie . . . Robbie Stewart.
Alexandra:	I'm Alexandra Pappas. **How do you do?**[7] Your brother left his bag of film on the ferryboat. I found it.
Robbie:	I'm really glad to see you. I mean . . . my brother'll be really glad to see you!
Ellen:	*[calling]* Robbie! Who is it?
Robbie:	It's Richard's film! I mean, Alexandra Pappas. *[to Alexandra]* Come in, please.
Richard:	Alexandra!
Alexandra:	Hello, Richard. I found your bag!
Richard:	Oh, thank you! Thank you! Um... Alexandra, let me introduce you. **This is**[8] my wife Marilyn.
Alexandra:	Richard showed me your photo. How do you do?
Marilyn:	Oh yes. Richard told us all about you. **It's nice to meet you.**[9]
Richard:	And this is my mother, Ellen Stewart.
Alexandra:	How do you do?
Richard:	And my father, Dr. Philip Stewart.
Philip:	Nice to meet you, Alexandra.
Richard:	And . . . ah . . . you met Robbie.
Alexandra:	Yes. And you must be Susan. Hi.
Susan:	Hi. Welcome.
Richard	I'm so glad you found the bag and took the time and trouble to return it.
Alexandra:	Oh, it was no trouble. I just took the wrong train.
Ellen:	Would you like something to eat?
Alexandra:	Thank you, no. I'm late for dinner at my house. I really have to go.
Richard:	Would you like to call home?
Alexandra:	I'd appreciate that.
Ellen:	Please, use the phone.
Alexandra:	Thanks. **Excuse me.**[10]
Richard:	*[to Robbie]* Alexandra's a high-school exchange student from Greece.
Robbie:	Where does she live?
Richard:	With a family in the Bronx.
Robbie:	Oh, that's not too far from here!
Richard:	**Take it easy,**[11] Robbie.
Alexandra:	Thank you. I can only stay a few minutes.

[7] **How do you do?**
This is a formal expression to say after someone introduces you.

[8] **This is . . .**
Use this phrase to introduce people. You may also say, *I'd like you to meet . . .*

[9] **It's nice to meet you.**
Use this expression after someone introduces you. It is less formal than *How do you do?*

[10] **Excuse me.**
Use this polite phrase before you walk away from someone.

[11] **Take it easy.** = Relax; be calm.

U.S. LIFE

Usually, when men or women meet someone for the first time, they shake hands and say, "It's nice to meet you." The formal form "How do you do?" is much less frequent. Asking about jobs or studies is a typical way to begin a conversation after meeting someone for the first time.

☞ YOUR TURN

• When you meet someone for the first time, do you always shake hands?

• What topics do you usually talk about with that person?

Ellen:	Have some iced tea.
Alexandra:	Thanks, Mrs. Stewart.
Robbie:	Please sit down, Alexandra.
Philip:	So, you're an exchange student. Where do you go to school?
Alexandra:	At the Bronx High School of Science.
Philip:	Oh, that's a very good school. What are your favorite subjects?
Alexandra:	Biology and mathematics. Richard tells me you're a doctor.
Philip:	Yes, a **pediatrician.**[12] And **what does your father do?**[13]
Alexandra:	He's a lawyer, in Thessaloniki.
Robbie:	Would you like some pasta? I made it myself. It might be a little cold.
Alexandra:	Thanks, no. I **do**[14] have to go. It was nice meeting you all.
Marilyn:	Well, maybe you'll come for lunch some Sunday, so we can really thank you for bringing Richard's bag back.
Alexandra:	Maybe.
Ellen:	You're welcome anytime. *[She and Richard walk with Alexandra to the front door.]*
Philip:	Good-bye.
Richard:	Can I drive you home?
Alexandra:	No, thanks. The train is just up the street. It won't take me long at all.
Richard:	Well, **you really saved the day for me,**[15] Alexandra.
Alexandra:	Bye.
Richard:	Bye-bye.
Ellen:	Good night.

[Alexandra leaves.]

Philip:	She's a smart young lady, and very nice.
Robbie:	Very! *[He sees Alexandra's bag on the chair.]* Hey, she forgot her bag!
Ellen:	I guess we'll be seeing Alexandra again. Right, Robbie?

END OF ACT III

[12] **pediatrician:** a childrens' doctor

[13] **What does your father do?** = What is your father's job?

[14] **do**
Here, *do* means "really."

[15] **You really saved the day for me.** = You really helped me a lot.

ACT III

Activities

Here are some activities to help you check your understanding of this episode.

INTRODUCTIONS

Usually, there is more than one way to say something. Choose *two* possible sentences for each of the following situations. Circle the letters of the *two* correct choices.

1. Richard wants to introduce himself to you. He says,
   a. "I'm Richard."
   b. "My name is Richard."
   c. "I'd like you to meet Richard."
2. Richard wants to introduce Marilyn to you. He says,
   a. "It's nice to meet you, Marilyn."
   b. "This is Marilyn."
   c. "I'd like you to meet Marilyn."
3. Robbie introduces Alexandra to you. She says,
   a. "It's nice to meet you."
   b. "How do you do?"
   c. "This is Robbie."
4. After meeting Alexandra and having an interesting conversation with her, you have to leave. You say,
   a. "It was a pleasure meeting you."
   b. "It was nice meeting you."
   c. "How do you do?"

TRAVELING BAGS

Richard's bag and Alexandra's bag traveled far today. Which route did their bags take? Circle a, b, or c to show the right travel sequence of their bags.

"The Blind Date"

ACT I

ACT II

ACT III

In this episode, you will study. . .

VOCABULARY

ma'am	firm
reservation	stomachache
starving	nervous
CPA	occasionally

GRAMMAR AND EXPRESSIONS

following directions
making polite suggestions
offering and ordering food
changing the subject

PRONUNCIATION

saying telephone numbers

 U.S. LIFE

• Do Americans like international foods?
• What kinds of jobs do most Americans have?

☞ **YOUR TURN**

• Did you ever have a blind date?
• Were you ever a baby-sitter?

Here is the complete script with study material for Episode 2. Use these materials before *or* after you watch.

ACT I

On a street in downtown Manhattan. Harry Bennett is carrying some flowers. He takes out a piece of paper from his pocket. It reads, "Susan Stewart, 83 Wooster Street, phone #555-9470, 8:00 P.M." Harry stops to talk to a street vendor.[1] **He asks him for directions.**

Harry: Excuse me. Can you help me?

Vendor: Sure, **what do you want?**[2]

Harry: Where is 83 Wooster Street?

Vendor: That's easy. *[He points.]* Walk to the corner. Then **make a left turn.**[3] Then walk two blocks to the **traffic light.**[4] Make another left to Wooster.

Harry: Thank you. To the corner and then a left?

Vendor: **Yeah.**[5] A left. **Hot dog?**[6] Only seventy-five cents.

Harry: No. Thank you. I have a dinner **date.**[7]

A little later. Harry is still lost. He goes to a pay phone and dials Susan's telephone number.

Harry: 555-9470 . . . and it's busy. . . .Try again. 555-9470 . . . and it's still busy. *[He walks to a grocery store to ask for directions.]* Excuse me, **ma'am.**[8] I'm looking for 83 Wooster Street.

Woman: Yes. Wooster Street is two **blocks,**[9] and 83 is to the right, about two houses.

Harry: Thank you, thank you!

Woman: You're welcome.

---

[1] **street vendor**
A *street vendor* sells food or other things on the street.

[2] **What do you want?**
The informal pronunciation is *Waddayawant?*

[3] **Make a left turn.** = Turn to the left.

[4] **traffic light:**

[5] **Yeah.** = Yes.
This is an informal word.

[6] **hot dog:** a frankfurter

[7] **date:** a plan to meet someone at a specific time

[8] **ma'am:** madam
Use *ma'am* when you speak directly to a woman and you don't know her name. To a young woman, you say *miss*. To a man, you say *sir*.

[9] **blocks:** streets

A few minutes later. Harry finds Wooster Street. He rings the buzzer to Susan's apartment.

Susan: *[at the **intercom**]*[10] Who is it?

Harry: Harry Bennett. Is this Susan?

Susan: Yes, it is. Come up. I'm on the top floor.

Susan: *[She opens the door.]* Hello, Harry. It's nice to meet you.

Harry: **Nice to meet you,**[11] Susan. *[He gives her the flowers.]* Sorry I'm late. The **traffic.**[12] The **parking.**[13] I was lost.

Susan: **What pretty flowers!**[14] Thank you. Oh, please come in. Don't worry about being late. It's fine. **Excuse the mess.**[15] I **just**[16] moved here. Oh, I'd like you to meet my **sister-in-law**[17] Marilyn. Marilyn Stewart, this is Harry Bennett.

Harry: **Pleased to meet you.**[18]

Marilyn: Nice to meet you, Harry.

Harry: Are we too late for our dinner **reservation?**[19]

Susan: No, the restaurant will hold our table. I know the owner very well. I eat there a lot.

[10] **intercom:**

[11] **Nice to meet you.** = It's nice to meet you.
Use this expression when you meet someone for the first time.

[12] **traffic:** many cars on the road

[13] **parking:** trying to find a place to leave the car

[14] **What pretty flowers!** = The flowers are very pretty.

[15] **Excuse the mess.** = I'm sorry that things are not neat.

[16] **just:** recently; a short time ago

[17] **sister-in-law:** a brother's wife

[18] **Pleased to meet you.** = Nice to meet you.
The complete form is *I'm pleased to meet you*.

[19] **reservation:** an arrangement to hold a table in a restaurant for a specific time
You also *make reservations* for hotel rooms, theater tickets, and airline tickets.

 ## U.S. LIFE

Susan and Harry are on a **blind date**. They don't know each other, and this is their first meeting. Blind dates are common in the United States. A friend or a member of the family often arranges this kind of date.

☞ YOUR TURN

- Are blind dates common in your country?
- Did you ever have a blind date or arrange one for someone else?

Harry:	Do you know the phone number of the restaurant? I'd like to call home and leave the number with the **baby-sitter.**[20]
Susan:	Sure. The number is . . . **five five five . . . seventeen twenty.**[21]
Harry:	May I use the phone?

[Susan indicates yes.]

Harry:	**Five five five . . . one seven two oh.**[22] Hello? Hi, Michelle. It's Daddy. Can I speak to Betty? I want to leave the phone number of the restaurant. . . . Hi, Betty. I'll be at five five five . . . seventeen twenty. OK. Thanks. See you later. *[He hangs up.]* Well, that's done. **Shall we**[23] go?
Susan:	I'm ready. See you later, Marilyn.
Marilyn:	Have a nice evening.
Harry:	Bye, Marilyn. **Hope to see you again.**[24]
Marilyn:	Me, too. Have **fun!**[25]
Susan:	Thanks.
Harry:	**After you.**[26]

END OF ACT I

[20] **baby-sitter**
Parents pay a *baby-sitter* to watch a child while they are away from home.

[21] **five five five . . . seventeen twenty**
This is one way to say the telephone number 555-1720.

[22] **five five five . . . one seven two oh**
This is another way to say the telephone number 555-1720. Pronounce the first three numbers of a telephone number by saying one number at a time. Say the last four numbers individually *or* in two parts.

[23] **Shall we . . . ?**
Use *Shall I* or *Shall we* to make a suggestion. This is a polite use.

[24] **Hope to see you again.** = I hope to see you again. Use this expression when you say good-bye to a new friend.

[25] **fun:** a good time

[26] **After you.** = I will go after you. This is a polite expression.

U.S. LIFE

Harry's daughter Michelle stays with a baby-sitter while Harry is on a date with Susan. It is common for American parents to pay a baby-sitter to watch their children for an evening. Teenage girls and boys often work as baby-sitters to earn money after school.

☞ YOUR TURN

- Do parents in your country often hire baby-sitters?
- Were you ever a baby-sitter?

Here are some activities to help you check your understanding of Act I.

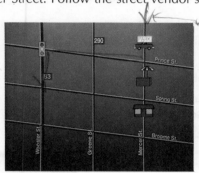

FOLLOWING DIRECTIONS

How should Harry walk from the street vendor to Susan's apartment? On the map, draw a line from Harry to 83 Wooster Street. Follow the street vendor's directions.

Walk to the corner. Then make a left turn. Then walk two blocks to the traffic light. Make another left to Wooster.

HARRY'S STEPS

What was the order of Harry's actions in Act I? In each circle, write the letter of the correct sentence to show the sequence of Harry's actions. The first answer is given.

a. He asked a woman for directions.

b. He tried to telephone Susan.

c. He found Susan's apartment.

d. He called the baby-sitter.

e. He asked Susan for the telephone number of the restaurant.

f. He left for the restaurant with Susan.

g. He asked a street vendor for directions.

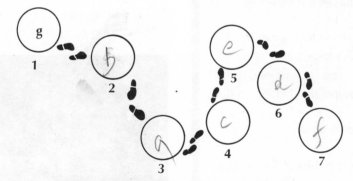

CHOOSE YOUR WORDS

For each situation, choose the more *polite* sentence. Circle *a* or *b*.

1. You meet someone for the first time. Immediately after the introduction you say,
   a. "Pleased to meet you."   **b.** "Yeah, nice to meet you."

2. You are walking out the door with a friend. You say,
   a. "You go first."   **b.** "After you."

3. Your friend is visiting your home, and you are feeling warm. You say,
   a. "May I open a window?"   **b.** "Can I open a window?"

4. You are watching television with a friend. You want to suggest a program, so you say,
   a. "Shall we watch *Family Album, U.S.A.?*"   **b.** "I think we should watch *Family Album, U.S.A.*"

ACT II

In a Thai restaurant[1] **later that evening. Somsak, the owner of the restaurant, greets Susan and Harry.**

Somsak: Ah! Miss Stewart! Welcome! How are you?

Susan: Fine, Somsak. And you?

Somsak: Fine, thank you.

Susan: This is my friend Harry Bennett.

Harry: Pleased to meet you.

Somsak: Very nice to meet you. Any friend of Miss Stewart's is welcome at Somsak's. Follow me, please.

Harry: *[to Susan]* I like it here.

Susan: I do, too. I come here often.

Somsak: A special place for special people.

Susan: Thank you, Somsak.

[Somsak leaves.]

Harry: Well! Nice restaurant.

Somsak: *[He returns.]* **Would you like[2]** something to drink?

Susan: Yes, **I'd like[3]** a glass of ginger ale with ice. Harry, what would you like?

Harry: Do you have a dry white wine?

Somsak: **How about[4]** a California chablis?

Harry: Chablis is fine.

Somsak: What would you like to eat?

Susan: I'd like the **mee krob.[5]** Harry, would you like to see a menu?

Harry: No, it's OK. **I'll have[6]** the mee krob also. *[to Susan]* What is it?

Susan: Crispy fried noodles. I love them.

Somsak: **May I bring you[7]** a salad?

Susan: Oh yes. What do you recommend today?

Somsak: I recommend rose-petal salad. Special for new friends.

Susan: *[to Harry]* Rose-petal salad?

Harry: Why not?

Somsak: **I'll take care of everything.[8]** *[He leaves.]*

Susan: I hope you're hungry.

Harry: What? Oh, yes. **Starving.[9]** Well, I . . .

Susan: *[at the same time]* Well, I . . .

U.S. LIFE

People in the United States often eat international foods. Chinese, Italian, Mexican, and Japanese restaurants are especially popular. In New York City you can find the food of most nations in the world.

[1] **Thai restaurant**
This restaurant serves food from the country of *Thailand*.

[2] **Would you like . . . ?** = Do you want . . . ?
Use this phrase *to offer* food or a drink.

[3] **I'd like . . .** = I want . . .
Use this phrase *to order* food or a drink.

[4] **How about . . . ?**
This phrase is another way *to offer*.

[5] **mee krob:** a popular Thai dish

[6] **I'll have . . .**
This phrase is another way to order.

[7] **May I bring you . . . ?**
This phrase is another way to offer.

[8] **I'll take care of everything.** = I'll get everything for you.

[9] **starving:** very hungry

☞ YOUR TURN

• Are there many international restaurants in your country?

• What is your favorite international food?

Harry:	What do you do at Universe Toy Company?
Susan:	I'm the **vice-president of new toy development.**[10]
Harry:	Terrific!
Susan:	I know you're a **CPA.**[11]
Harry:	That's true. Harry Bennett, certified public accountant. I love numbers. I do some work for Smith and Dale, your company's accounting **firm.**[12]
Susan:	And so . . .
Harry:	Here we are.
Susan:	Yes.
Harry:	I have a daughter.
Susan:	I know. How old is she?
Harry:	She's nine years old.
Susan:	That's a nice age. What's her name?
Harry:	Michelle.
Susan:	Do you have a picture of her?

[Harry shows her a photo.]

Susan:	She's very pretty.
Harry:	Thank you.
Somsak:	*[He arrives with the salad.]* Rose-petal salad. And there's a phone call for you, Mr. Bennett.
Harry:	Excuse me, Susan. *[He leaves the table.]*
Susan:	*[to Somsak]* I hope nothing is wrong.
Somsak:	I'll get the rest of the dinner. Excuse me. *[He leaves.]*
Harry:	*[He returns.]* **Please forgive me,**[13] Susan, but . . . I have to leave. I feel terrible, but . . .
Susan:	**What's the matter?**[14]
Harry:	My daughter isn't feeling well.
Susan:	Oh no! Is it serious?
Harry:	I don't know. The baby-sitter says she has a **stomachache,**[15] and she's crying. I'll have to go home. Will you forgive me?
Susan:	Of course. I'm so sorry for Michelle. And you didn't have a chance to eat.
Harry:	Oh, it's OK. Let me take you home first.
Susan:	No, no. Please, go ahead.
Harry:	It's our first date.
Susan:	We'll make another. Please don't worry.
Harry:	*[He gets up to leave.]* I'll phone you.
Susan:	I hope your daughter is all right. Good-bye.
Harry:	Good-bye.

END OF ACT II

10 vice-president of new toy development
People bring Susan ideas for new toys. She has an important job in the company.

toys

11 CPA: certified public accountant
An *accountant* keeps business records. To become a CPA, an accountant must pass a government test.

12 firm: a business company.

13 Please forgive me. = I'm sorry.

14 What's the matter? = What's the problem?

15 stomachache: a pain in the stomach
The pronunciation of *ch* in this word sounds like *k*.

ACT II

Activities

Here are some activities to help you check your understanding of Act II.

OFFERING AND ORDERING

Here is a menu from an American restaurant. Imagine that you want to order lunch. Use the phrase **I'd like** or **I'll have**.

Would you like something to drink?

SANDWICHES

MEAT:
FRESH TURKEY . . . 5.65
ROAST BEEF 5.45
CORNED BEEF 5.45
BOILED HAM 4.40
SALAMI 4.25

SALADS:
TUNA SALAD 4.25
CHICKEN SALAD . . . 4.25
EGG SALAD 3.20

CHEESE:
AMERICAN CHEESE . . 3.20
SWISS CHEESE . . . 3.45
HAM & SWISS 4.95
GRILLED AMERICAN
CHEESE 3.40

ICE CREAM

ICE CREAM
  ONE SCOOP 1.50
  TWO SCOOPS . . . 2.25
ICE CREAM SODAS . . 2.45
ICE CREAM SUNDAES 2.95
(VANILLA, STRAWBERRY, CHOCOLATE,)
COFFEE

BEVERAGES [beverids] 飲料

COLA, DIET COLA . . . 1.10
MILK SHAKE 2.25
FRESH LEMONADE . . . 1.75
COFFEE 70
TEA 70
HERBAL TEA 85
(6 FLAVORS)

GETTING TO KNOW HIM

A. Before Harry left the restaurant, Susan learned some things about his life. Try to complete the following sentences. If necessary, you can read Act II again to find the information.

accountant [ə'kauntənt]

Harry Bennett works as an _____. He is a CPA, and he loves _numbers_. Harry has a _daughter_. Her name is _michelle_. She is _nine_ years old.

B. Now complete these sentences with true information about *yourself*.
I work as a(n) ___housewife___.
I love ___cooking___.

Write about someone in your family.
My ___husband___'s name is ___Young xiong___. zhào
___He___ is ___58___ years old.

ORDER, PLEASE

What is the correct order of events in Act II? Write the number *1, 2, 3, 4,* or *5* on each of the lines to show the correct sequence. The first answer is given.

_3_ **a.** Harry shows Susan a picture of his daughter.

_4_ **b.** There is a telephone call for Harry.

_5_ **c.** Harry leaves the restaurant.

_1_ **d.** Susan introduces Harry to Somsak.

_2_ **e.** Susan and Harry order dinner.

ACT III

In Susan's apartment. Susan and her sister-in-law Marilyn are eating the food from the Thai restaurant.

Marilyn: What happened?

Susan: The baby-sitter called. His daughter is sick.

Marilyn: What's wrong?

Susan: I think she has a stomachache. He's a good father.

Marilyn: So . . . what do you think of him?

Susan: He's very nice. But I think he was **nervous**[1] tonight. It was his first date in two years.

Marilyn: Will you see him again?

Susan: I hope so.

Marilyn: This food is delicious.

Susan: He didn't get a thing to eat.

Marilyn: *[She looks at the food on the table.]* You ordered enough for three or four people, but **I'm not complaining.**[2] The food is delicious.

[There is a knock at the door.]

Susan: Who is that?

Marilyn: Do you think it's . . .

Susan: No. *[She goes to the door and looks through the **peephole.**[3]]* You won't believe it, Marilyn!

Marilyn: I believe it. Even without looking.

[Susan opens the door.]

Harry: Hi!

Susan: **How . . . ?**[4]

Harry: Your downstairs neighbor let me in.

Susan: Did you go home?

Harry: I did, but everything is OK, so I decided to come back. To **apologize**[5] for leaving so early, I brought you a little gift. *[He gives her a plant.]* It's a **bonsai tree**[6] for your new apartment. Hi, Marilyn. I hope it's not too late.

Marilyn: Oh, not at all. We're still eating.

[1] **nervous:** not calm; upset

[2] **I'm not complaining.** = It's not a problem for me. This is an informal expression.

[3] **peephole:**

[4] **How . . . ?**
Susan doesn't complete her question. Harry understands that she means "How did you get inside the building?"

[5] **apologize:** to say you're sorry

[6] **bonsai tree:**

Susan:	Please, come in. Join us. It's our meal from the restaurant. And how is your daughter?
Harry:	Oh, she's fine. It was only a **tummy**[7] ache.
Susan:	It's good that you went back.
Harry:	Yes, I think it's important for me to be there since her mother died.
Susan:	I agree. Aren't you hungry?
Harry:	**As a matter of fact**[8]. . . I *am* hungry.
Marilyn:	There's lots of food left.
Harry:	*[eating]* Mmm, this is delicious!
Susan:	Enjoy!
Marilyn:	I'm going to excuse myself. *[She gets up.]* I have a lot of work to do to get ready for tomorrow. Good night, Harry. It was nice meeting you.
Harry:	Bye, Marilyn.
Marilyn:	Good night, Susan.
Susan:	Good night, Marilyn.

[Marilyn leaves.]

Susan:	She's going to a **fashion show**[9] here in the city tomorrow. She is sleeping here so she won't have to travel from Riverdale in the morning.
Harry:	You two must be **close.**[10]
Susan:	We are. The whole Stewart family is close.
Harry:	I like that.

Later that evening . . .

Harry:	And then, two years ago, my wife died.
Susan:	You miss her.
Harry:	I do . . . yes, but I have Michelle . . . and with time . . .
Susan:	**Is there anyone else in your life?**[11]
Harry:	No, not yet. What about you?
Susan:	Oh, I date **occasionally,**[12] but my work keeps me busy.
Harry:	*[He looks at his watch.]* Ooh, **speaking of**[13] keeping busy—I have an early start tomorrow, and the baby-sitter has to get home. *[He starts to put on his jacket.]* **Where did the time go?**[14] It's **midnight.**[15] Thank you, Susan. I had a nice evening.
Susan:	Me, too, Harry. *[She walks with him to the door.]* Harry?

[7] **tummy:** stomach
This is an informal word. Children often say *tummy* instead of *stomach*.

[8] **As a matter of fact . . .** = It is true . . .

[9] **fashion show:**

[10] **close:** very friendly with each other

[11] **Is there anyone else in your life?**
Here, Susan means, "Do you have a special woman, or girlfriend, in your life?"

[12] **occasionally:** sometimes; not often

[13] **speaking of**
Use this expression to change the subject in a conversation.

[14] **Where did the time go?** = The time passed very quickly.

[15] **midnight:** twelve o'clock at night

Harry:	Yes?
Susan:	I'd like to meet your daughter someday.
Harry:	Does that mean that I can see you again?
Susan:	Of course.
Harry:	Wonderful. I'll call you, and we'll go out to dinner.
Susan:	Please do. [wound]
Harry:	I promise I won't leave early.
Susan:	It was for a good reason.
Harry:	**You know something?**[16]
Susan:	What?
Harry:	I think we're **going to**[17] be good friends. Good night, Susan.
Susan:	Good night, Harry. **Have a safe trip home.**[18] *[She closes the door. A moment later there is a loud sound in the hall. Susan opens the door.]* Are you all right?
Harry:	*[He fell over the* **umbrella stand,**[19] *and now he is picking it up.]* Sorry.
Susan:	*[She smiles.]* **I never liked that umbrella stand.**[20] Good night, Harry.

END OF ACT III

[16] **You know something?** = Do you know something? This expression means "I really want to say this to you."

[17] **going to**
Harry says *gonna*. This is the informal pronunciation of the future tense with *going to*.

[18] **Have a safe trip home.**
You can use this expression when you say good-bye.

[19] **umbrella stand:**

[20] **I never liked that umbrella stand.**
To make a situation less serious, you can use the expression *I never liked _____* or *I never liked _____, anyway*. For example, imagine that a dish falls and breaks. Instead of making someone feel bad about it, you might just say, *I never liked that dish, anyway.*

U.S. LIFE

In the United States, about 5% of all jobs are in agriculture, fishing, and mining. About 25% are in manufacturing and construction. The rest of the jobs are in service professions, such as teaching, selling, and medicine.

☞ YOUR TURN

- Do you have a job? If so, what is it? Which other occupation might you like to have?
- Which occupations in your country are more usual for men than for women? Which jobs are more usual for women?

ACT III *Activities*

Here are some activities to help you check your understanding of this episode.

OCCUPATIONS

Write the name of each person's job on the line below each picture. The first answer is given.

1. _____vendor_____

3. _____

5. _nurse_____

2. _account____

4. _Teacher____

6. _____

DATE LINE

Harry had a busy evening. Draw a line to show the correct order of events.

Begin here.   *End here.*

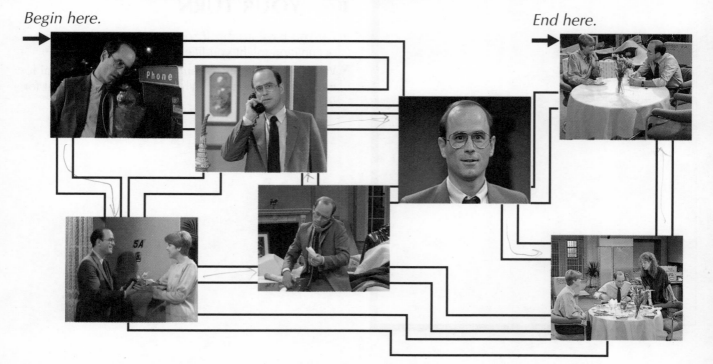

EPISODE 3

"Grandpa's Trunk"

ACT I

In this episode, you will study . . .

VOCABULARY [və'kæbjuləri]

trunk	mile
stuff	destination
hanger	anniversary
aisle	belongings

GRAMMAR AND EXPRESSIONS

simple present tense for future schedules
the preposition *by* 에 의하여
two-word verbs
sentences ending with *too*

[sedju:l]
skedju:l

ACT II

PRONUNCIATION

intonation: *either/or* questions
stress: *fifty/fifteen*

U.S. LIFE

- When do Americans retire?
- Where do older Americans live?

☞ YOUR TURN

- Is there a retirement age in your country?
- In your country, do grandparents usually live with their children and grandchildren?

ACT III

Here is the complete script with study material for Episode 3. Use these materials before *or* after you watch.

ACT I

In the Stewarts' house one morning. Ellen and Marilyn are preparing breakfast in the kitchen.

Ellen: *[She takes the **tea kettle**[1] off the stove.]* Marilyn, **you want coffee or tea?**[2]

Marilyn: Coffee, please.

Ellen: I am so **excited!**[3] At this time tomorrow morning, Grandpa **will be sitting**[4] in the kitchen with us.

Marilyn: **When does he arrive?**[5]

Ellen: At six o'clock this evening.

Marilyn: **By plane?**[6]

Ellen: No, **by train.**[7]

Marilyn: Are we **picking him up**[8] at the station?

Ellen: Not Grandpa. He doesn't want anybody picking him up. He likes to be independent.

Marilyn: **Huh.**[9]

Ellen: Oh, let's go upstairs and prepare Grandpa's room.

Marilyn: Great! Let's do it!

[1] **tea kettle:**

[2] **You want coffee or tea?** = Do you want coffee or tea? This is an *either/or* question, a question that asks for a choice between two things. In this kind of question, use a rising *and* a rising-and-falling intonation. The voice goes up on the first item *(coffee)*; the voice goes up and then down on the second item *(tea)*:

Do you want coffee or tea?

[3] **excited:** nervous but happy about something.

[4] **will be sitting**
Use the progressive *(-ing)* verb tenses for an action that begins before and ends after a specific time. *At this time tomorrow morning*, Grandpa will be in the middle of sitting in the kitchen with the family.

[5] **When does he arrive?** = When will he arrive? You can use the simple present tense to refer to future schedules. A *schedule* is a list of times for certain things to happen.

[6] **by plane;** [7] **by train**
Use the preposition *by* with ways to travel: *by* car, *by* boat, *by* bus, *by* taxi.

[8] **picking (him) up:** going to get (him)
Pick up is a two-word verb. The word *up* is necessary for the meaning. If the direct object is a pronoun *(him)*, it always comes between the two words. But if the direct object is not a pronoun, it may come before *or* after the two-word verb: *Pick Grandpa up* and *pick up Grandpa* are both correct.

[9] **Huh.**
Here, this sound shows that Marilyn is thinking.

[Ellen and Marilyn get up to leave. Richard and Robbie enter the kitchen.]

Richard:	Good morning, Mom.
Robbie:	**Morning.**[10]
Ellen:	Well, hi, **fellas.**[11]
Richard:	Hello.
Marilyn:	Hi, **honey.**[12]
Richard & Robbie:	Morning, Marilyn.
Marilyn:	We're going upstairs to **set up**[13] Grandpa's room. There's coffee ready.

[Ellen and Marilyn go upstairs. Richard and Robbie begin to make breakfast.]

Robbie:	I'm really excited about seeing Grandpa.
Richard:	Me, too. *[to Robbie]* Milk, please.
Robbie:	He's so funny. He always makes me laugh. I hope Grandpa's going to like living with us.
Richard:	I think he will. It just takes time to feel comfortable in a new place.
Robbie:	Won't he **miss**[14] being in Florida?
Richard:	Well, he will. But I think he'll like being here with the family.
Robbie:	Are you sure about that? It's crazy here most of the time.
Richard:	But it's fun.
Robbie:	**That's for sure.**[15]
Richard:	You know, maybe I'll put together some photos of Grandpa as a "welcome" present.
Robbie:	That's a **neat**[16] idea. What can I do? *[He thinks.]* **I've got it!**[17] I have a picture of Grandpa and Dad and me in my wallet. It's from the Fathers and Sons' Breakfast at my **junior high school**[18] **graduation.**[19] *[He takes out his wallet and shows the picture to Richard.]*
Richard:	*[He looks at the picture.]* Oh, I remember this picture.
Robbie:	I'd really like to pick up Grandpa at the **railroad**[20] station.

[10] **Morning.** = Good morning.

[11] **fellas:** fellows
Fellows means "men" or "boys."
It is an informal word.

[12] **honey:** darling; dear
Use this word to show that you feel close to someone. *Honey* is sometimes used by a woman to a man, by a man to a woman, or by a woman to another woman. It is never used by a man to another man.

[13] **set up:** to prepare; make ready
Set up, like *pick up*, is a two-word verb.
Marilyn says, ". . . *set up* Grandpa's room."
She might also say, "*set* Grandpa's room *up*."

[14] **miss:** to feel sad when remembering something you liked or loved and don't have now

[15] **That's for sure.** = I agree with you about that.
This is an informal expression.

[16] **neat:** great; fine
This is an informal word.

[17] **I've got it!** = I have an idea!

[18] **junior high school**
Students attend *junior high school* after the sixth grade of elementary school. *Junior high school* includes grades 7, 8, and 9.

[19] **graduation:** completing studies at a school

[20] **railroad:** train

"It's from the Fathers and Sons' Breakfast at my junior high school graduation."

Richard: Railroad stations or airports—Grandpa always tells us he'll get here **by himself.**[21]

Robbie: He's **something!**[22]

Upstairs in the Stewarts' home. Ellen and Marilyn are preparing Grandpa's room.

Marilyn: *[She points to the **trunk**.[23]]* Is this all Grandpa's stuff?

Ellen: That's it. But I'm sure he has a few **bags**[24] with him on the train.

Marilyn: What's inside?

Ellen: I don't know. It's locked.

Philip: *[He enters.]* Hi.

Ellen: Oh, hi, darling.

Marilyn: Morning, Philip.

Philip: I want to put some of my good **hangers**[25] in Grandpa's closet. You know I'm very excited about his arrival.

Ellen: **We are, too.**[26] Susan called early this morning. She's unhappy because she's had to go to Chicago on a business trip and can't leave **till**[27] tonight. She wants to be here for Grandpa.

Philip: Well, Grandpa will be **disappointed,**[28] too. He loves Susan. **She always reminds him of Grandma.**[29] Well, how's everything here?

Marilyn: Fine. We were just **wondering**[30] about this trunk.

Ellen: It's locked.

Philip: Oh. *[He takes a key from his pocket.]* I have the key. Grandpa sent it to me. *[He tries to put the key into the lock of the trunk.]*

END OF ACT I

[21] **by himself:** alone
With *by*, you can also use *myself, yourself, herself, itself, ourselves, yourselves,* and *themselves.*

[22] **something:** great; wonderful
This is an informal use.

[23] **trunk:**

[24] **bags:** suitcases

[25] **hangers:**

[26] **We are, too.** = We also are very excited.
When *too* is at the end of a sentence, you sometimes do not repeat every word in the phrase or sentence before it. Here is another example:

Ellen wants to prepare Grandpa's room, and Marilyn does, too.

In this sentence, *does* means "wants to prepare Grandpa's room."

[27] **till:** until

[28] **disappointed:** not satisfied; feeling that something is not as you hoped or wished

[29] **She always reminds him of Grandma.** = Susan always makes him think of Grandma because Susan looks like her.

[30] **wondering:** asking ourselves; thinking

ACT I

Activities

Here are some activities to help you check your understanding of Act I.

OPINIONS AND BELIEFS

What do you think? Read each sentence about Grandpa. Then circle *a* or *b* to show a logical opinion or belief.

1. Ellen: He doesn't want anybody picking him up.
   a. I guess he's independent.
   b. I guess he's not a happy person.

2. Robbie: He's so funny.
   a. I bet he doesn't like to laugh.
   b. I bet people laugh when they are with him.

3. **Richard:** . . . I think he'll like being here with the family.
   a. I suppose he enjoys being with them.
   b. I suppose he doesn't want to live with them.

LOOK WHO'S TALKING

Who said each of the following sentences? Write the *number* of each sentence in the box below the picture of the correct speaker. If necessary, look back at the script for Act I to find the answers. The first answer is given.

1. "At this time tomorrow morning, Grandpa will be sitting in the kitchen with us."
2. "I hope Grandpa's going to like living with us."
3. "You know, maybe I'll put together some photos of Grandpa as a 'welcome' present."
4. "I want to put some of my good hangers in Grandpa's closet."
5. "We were just wondering about this trunk."

Philip
[ ]

Ellen
[1]

Marilyn
[ ]

Richard
[ ]

Robbie
[ ]

ACT II

On an Amtrak[1] **train the same day. The train is traveling from Florida to New York City. Grandpa is sitting on the train. A woman puts her suitcase on the seat next to him.**

Elsa: Excuse me. **Is this seat taken?** [2]

Grandpa: No, it's not taken.

Elsa: Oh, thank you.

Grandpa: Oh, let me help you with this. *[He puts her suitcase in the overhead rack.]*

Elsa: Oh, thank you.

Grandpa: Do you want to sit **by** [3] the window?

Elsa: No, no, no. I like the **aisle** [4] seat better. Please, you sit by the window.

[They sit down.]

Grandpa: My name is Stewart . . . Malcolm Stewart. Pleased to meet you. *[They shake hands.]*

Elsa: I'm Elsa Tobin. How do you do?

Grandpa: Do you live in New York?

Elsa: No, no. I'm from Florida.

Grandpa: **I am, too.**[5] But didn't you just **get on?** [6]

Elsa: No, no. I just changed my seat. A man next to me was smoking, and smoke really bothers me. Where are you from in Florida?

Grandpa: Titusville. It's near Orlando.

Elsa: **Small world.**[7] I'm from Titusville, too.

Grandpa: Really? What part?

Elsa: My husband and I live near Spaceport.

Grandpa: I know that area. My house is only a few **miles** [8] from Spaceport. Do you still live there?

[1] **Amtrak:** a train company, with trains traveling between cities in the United States
The name Amtrak comes from the words **Am**erican, **tra**vel, and trac**k**.

[2] **Is this seat taken?** = Is someone sitting here?

[3] **by:** next to

[4] **aisle:** the place to walk between rows of seats
This word has exactly the same pronunciation as *I'll*.

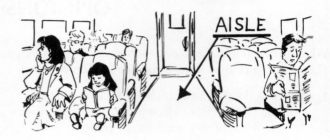

[5] **I am, too.** = I am from Florida, too.

[6] **get on:** to enter
You also *get on* a bus and a plane.

[7] **Small world.** = It's a small world.
You can use this expression if you are far from home and you meet someone who lives near you.

[8] **miles**
One kilometer = 0.6214 mile, or about 5/8 mile.

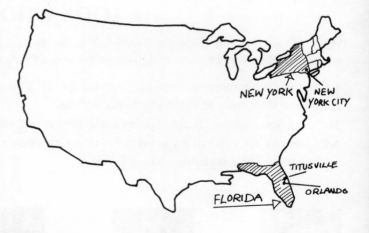

Elsa: Oh yes, yes. My husband's there now. He couldn't **take time off**[9] to come to New York with me. Do you still live there?

Grandpa: No. I sold the house and the furniture, put a few personal things in an old trunk, and **shipped**[10] it to my children in New York. That's my **destination.**[11]

Elsa: Are you married?

Grandpa: My wife died four years ago. She was a wonderful woman. A real friend.

Elsa: I'm sorry. Really, I'm sorry.

Grandpa: Lots of wonderful memories. We were married almost **fifty**[12] years. Well, forty-seven, **to be exact.**[13]

Elsa: John and I celebrate our fortieth **anniversary**[14] next month.

Grandpa: Oh, **congratulations!**[15] That's nice. What does John do?

Elsa: He's an aerospace engineer and works for Orlando Aircraft Corporation. He started with them almost forty years ago. What do you do?

Grandpa: I just **retired.**[16] **Had my own company.**[17] A **construction company.**[18] Roads,[19] bridges,[20] big stuff. But I just sold it and retired.

[A conductor walks over to them. He asks to see Mrs. Tobin's ticket.]

Conductor: Excuse me, ma'am. Ticket, please.

Elsa: *[to Grandpa]* **Would you kindly**[21] hold these keys, please? I have a ticket, I know. I was in the smoking section.

Conductor: It's OK, **lady.**[22] **Take your time.**[23]

[9] **take time off:** not go to work; stay away from work
Take off is a two-word verb.

[10] **shipped:** sent

[11] **destination:** the place where you plan to arrive at the end of a trip

[12] **fifty**
In *fifty*, only the first syllable is strong. In *fifteen*, both syllables are strong.

[13] **to be exact:** exactly

[14] **anniversary:** a wedding anniversary; the date someone was married

[15] **Congratulations!** = That's great!
Say *congratulations* to people when they tell you good news about themselves.

[16] **retired:** stopped working, usually because of old age

[17] **Had my own company.** = I had my own company.
This means that Grandpa was the owner of the company.

[18] **construction company:** a business for building things

[19] **roads:** streets; highways

[20] **bridges:**

[21] **Would you kindly . . . ?** = Please . . .
Use this phrase to begin a formal request.

[22] **lady:** woman
Unlike *ma'am*, this is not a very polite form.

[23] **Take your time.** = It is not necessary to hurry.

Grandpa: I'm sure it's in your **purse**,²⁴ Mrs. Tobin.

Elsa: Oh, here it is. *[She finds the ticket in her handbag and gives it to the conductor.]*

[The conductor moves on.]

Grandpa: And here are your keys.

Elsa: Thank you.

Grandpa: Do you have family in New York?

Elsa: No, no. But I do have very close friends in New York City. We like to go to the theater together. You said you have family in New York.

Grandpa: **Yes, indeed.**²⁵ A son and his wife and their three children—my grandchildren.

Elsa: You **must be** ²⁶ excited.

Grandpa: **I can't wait,**²⁷ to see them!

Elsa: Are you going to live with them?

Grandpa: Yes.

Elsa: **Permanently?** ²⁸

Grandpa: Well . . . they want me to, but it's too early to know for sure. I'm pretty independent. I tried to teach my **kids** ²⁹ the importance of independence, but I'm not sure I want to be alone. Some people don't **mind**³⁰ being alone. I do.

Elsa: I understand. But tell me. Why did you stop working?

Grandpa: I retired because . . . I wanted to be with my family. I didn't want to be alone anymore!

END OF ACT II

²⁴ **purse:** handbag; pocketbook

²⁵ **Yes, indeed.** = That's true.

²⁶ **must be:** obviously are

²⁷ **I can't wait!** = I am excited.

²⁸ **permanently:** with no plan to change

²⁹ **kids:** children
This is an informal word.

³⁰ **mind:** to care about

 ## U.S. LIFE

Many Americans retire at the age of 65. Some retire at a younger age, and others choose never to retire. The federal government provides **social security** (money each month) for workers who retire.

☞ YOUR TURN

- Is 65 the retirement age in your country?
- How do older people in your country get money after they stop working?

ACT II

Activities

Here are some activities to help you check your understanding of Act II.

PERSONAL INFORMATION

Here are some parts of the conversation between Grandpa and Elsa Tobin. On the blank lines, write the missing parts of their conversation. Choose the correct answers from the box.

1. Grandpa: My name is Stewart . . . Malcolm Stewart.
   _____.
   Elsa: I'm Elsa Tobin. How do you do?

2. Elsa: _____?
   Grandpa: My wife died four years ago.

3. Elsa: _____ in Florida?
   Grandpa: Titusville. It's near Orlando.

4. Elsa: John and I celebrate our fortieth anniversary next month.
   Grandpa: _____!

5. Grandpa: _____?
   Elsa: No, no. But I do have very close friends in New York City.

> Are you married
>
> Pleased to meet you
>
> Where are you from
>
> Do you have family in New York
>
> Congratulations

NEXT STOP. . .

Show the correct order of events in Grandpa's life. Write the *letter* of each sentence in the correct sign on the railroad track. The first answer is given.

> a. He left Florida.
> b. He sold his business and retired.
> c. He had a construction company.
> d. He sent a trunk to his family in New York.
> e. His wife died.

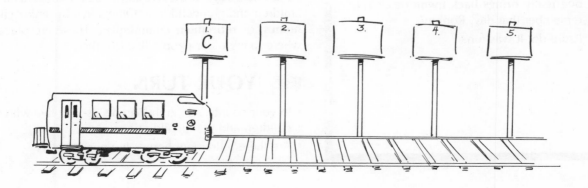

ACT III

On the Amtrak train later that day. The train is arriving in New York City.

Voice: Ladies and gentlemen, Amtrak is happy to announce our arrival in New York City. The train will be stopping in five minutes. Please check to be sure you have your **belongings.**[1] And have a good stay in **the Big Apple.**[2] Thanks.

Elsa: Well, here we are. It was so nice meeting you, Mr. Stewart.

Grandpa: And nice meeting you, too, Mrs. Tobin. Please **look us up.**[3] **We're in the phone book.**[4] Dr. Philip Stewart, in Riverdale.

Elsa: Your son?

Grandpa: That's right. And have a good time in New York.

Elsa: And don't be so independent. You're very lucky to have a caring family.

[Grandpa nods his head.]

In the Stewarts' living room that evening. The family is speaking with Grandpa after his long trip.

Robbie: When can we go fishing?

Grandpa: Robbie, we'll go fishing soon, and we'll take your dad with us.

Philip: I'm ready, Grandpa. **You name the day.**[5]

Ellen: That's a great idea, Grandpa! Philip needs **a day off.**[6]

Robbie: *[to Richard]* Let's give him our presents— now.

Richard: Good idea.

Grandpa: Presents—for me?

Richard: *[He gives his present to Grandpa.]* From me and Marilyn.

Robbie: And this one's from me. I looked **all over the house**[7] to find it.

Grandpa: *[He unwraps the presents. They contain photographs of him with the family.]* Richard, these are terrific pictures. This one really **brings back memories.**[8] You remember that day, Robbie?

Robbie: I sure do. It was fun.

[1] **belongings:** personal things

[2] **the Big Apple:** New York City

[3] **Look (us) up.** = Call or visit (us).
Look up is a two-word verb.

[4] **We're in the phone book.** = You can find our address and telephone number in the telephone book.

[5] **You name the day.** = Tell me which day.

[6] **a day off:** a day away from the job

[7] **all over the house:** everywhere in the house

[8] **brings back memories:** makes me think about past times.

 ## U.S. LIFE

Some older Americans live in the same house as their children and grandchildren. Others live in **senior citizen homes**, or **retirement communites**. These are places where many older people live together.

YOUR TURN

- In your country, do grandparents usually live with their children and grandchildren?
- Are there retirement homes in your country?

Grandpa:	*[He looks at a photo of himself and Susan.]* Oh, I'm sorry Susan isn't here. I miss her very much.
Ellen:	She feels bad, too, Grandpa. She called to say the plane was **delayed.**[9] You know airports.
Grandpa:	I can't wait to see her. She looks just like Grandma at that age. I'd better unpack. I started traveling twenty-four hours ago. *[He gets up.]* I'm not so young anymore.
Ellen:	Don't you want something to eat?
Grandpa:	No, thanks. After a good night's sleep, I'll enjoy breakfast even more.
Philip:	Well, come on, Dad. Ellen and I'll take you to your room.
Robbie:	I'm sure glad you're here, Grandpa.
Richard:	Good night, Grandpa.
Marilyn:	**Pleasant dreams.**[10]

[The family leaves the living room. Ellen, Philip, and Grandpa go upstairs to Grandpa's room.]

Grandpa:	Philip, do you have the key to the trunk?
Philip:	I have the key, but it doesn't work. *[He gives the key to Grandpa.]*
Grandpa:	*[He tries the key, but it doesn't unlock the trunk.]* I sent the wrong key. *[He then finds the right key in his pocket and unlocks the trunk.]* I have something for you. I made it myself. I think you'll enjoy it. *[He takes something from the trunk and gives it to Philip.]* I **researched**[11] it for over a year. It's our **family tree.**[12]
Ellen:	*[She looks at it.]* Oh, Grandpa! **How exciting!**[13]
Philip:	Fabulous! **Why,**[14] I didn't know that your grandfather was born in Germany.
Grandpa:	Lots of interesting information about our family. A gift from me.
Ellen:	Thank you so much. *[She hugs Grandpa.]*
Susan:	*[She rushes into the room.]* Grandpa! Grandpa! Oh, Grandpa, I'm so happy to see you! *[She hugs Grandpa.]*
Grandpa:	*[He looks at her.]* Oh, you look so beautiful, Susan. My granddaughter. Like I always said, you look just like Grandma.
Philip:	*[to Grandpa]* I think you're going to be very happy here with us.
Ellen:	I know you will.
Grandpa:	I don't feel alone anymore.

END OF ACT III

[9] **delayed:** made late

[10] **Pleasant dreams.** = Sleep well.
Use this phrase when someone is going to go to sleep.

[11] **researched:** studied carefully to get facts and information

[12] **family tree:** a chart of a person's family history

[13] **How exciting!** = That's very exciting.

[14] **Why**
Why is not a question word here. *Why* at the beginning of a sentence sometimes shows surprise. This is a formal use.

ACT III
Activities

Here are some activities to help you check your understanding of this episode.

THE FAMILY TREE

Here is the Stewarts' family tree. What are the relationships among the people in the family? Refer to the family tree to complete the sentences. Choose your answers from the box. Write your answers on the blank lines.

husband	son	daughter	brother	sister	wife	grandson	sister-in-law

1. Philip is Malcolm's _____.
2. Susan is Marilyn's _____.
3. Richard is Malcolm's _____.
4. Robbie is Richard's _____.
5. Susan is Ellen's _____.
6. Ellen is Philip's _____.
7. Richard is Marilyn's _____.
8. Susan is Robbie's _____.

Malcolm Bernice

Philip Ellen

Marilyn Richard   Susan Robbie

The Stewarts

WHAT DO YOU SAY?

What might you say in each of the following conversations? Choose your answers from the box. Then write each answer on the correct line. Use each answer only once.

That's for sure I've got it	Small world Congratulations	Take your time I can't wait	Look me up Pleasant dreams

1. "I'll be in your city next month."
   "_____. Maybe we can have dinner together."
2. "I'm from Washington."
   "_____. I am, too."
3. "I found a wonderful new job last week."
   "_____!"
4. "This is a very interesting television program."
   "_____. There's nothing else like *Family Album, U.S.A.*"

5. "I'm still eating."
   "_____. We don't have to leave for another hour."
6. "Good night."
   "_____. I'll see you in the morning."
7. "I heard that you will be taking a vacation next month."
   "Yes,_____. I need some time off."
8. "It's Dad's birthday next week. What can we give him?"
   "_____! Let's make a family tree for him."

EPISODE 4

[handwritten: Sla Kingdom 王⁅国⁆]

ACT I

In this episode, you will study . . .

VOCABULARY

aerobics
kidding
bet
twist *[handwritten: 迅疠]*

GRAMMAR AND EXPRESSIONS

It's a snap.
No sweat.
It's a piece of cake.
How much? and *How many?*

ACT II

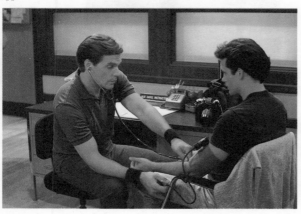

PRONUNCIATION

can (cn)
What do you . . . ? (Waddaya)
did you (didja)
don't you (dontcha)

 ## U.S. LIFE

What do Americans do to stay healthy?

☞ YOUR TURN

What kinds of exercises are popular in your country?

ACT III

"A Piece of Cake" ▶ 37

Here is the complete script with study material for Episode 4. Use these materials before *or* after you watch.

ACT I

Outside the Stewarts' house early Friday evening. Marilyn Stewart rides to the house on a bicycle. Inside, her husband Richard is looking at photos in his album. Marilyn enters and sits on the floor.

Marilyn:	I am **exhausted.**[1] My new exercise class is so hard.
Richard:	Your *new* exercise class?
Marilyn:	Yeah. My new **advanced**[2] exercise class.
Richard:	Why advanced?
Marilyn:	My instructor thought that the beginner's class was too easy for me.
Richard:	*[He laughs because she looks so tired.]* Too easy for you? *[He helps her stand up.]*
Marilyn:	Don't laugh. In the beginner's class, they give you a chance to rest between exercises.
Richard:	So?
Marilyn:	The advanced class is **nonstop.**[3]
Richard:	*[He **teases**[4] her.]* I lift weights every morning for sixty minutes without stopping. *[He shows her his arm muscle.]* **No problem.**[5]
Marilyn:	Listen, Richard, doing **aerobics**[6] for an hour is a lot **different than**[7] lifting weights.
Richard:	Yeah. Quite a bit different. I think aerobics is easy. **I could**[8] **work out**[9] in your class with no problem.
Marilyn:	You think so?
Richard:	Oh, **without a doubt.**[10] When's the next class?
Marilyn:	Tomorrow morning at ten o'clock. Try it.
Richard:	Tomorrow morning after lifting weights, I'll try aerobics. *[He snaps his fingers.]*

[1] **exhausted:** very tired

[2] **advanced:** more difficult

[3] **nonstop:** without stopping

[4] **teases:** annoys by joking with someone

[5] **No problem.** = It's easy.

[6] **aerobics:** exercises for good breathing and a strong heart

[7] **different than**
The better form is *different from*. Like Marilyn, some Americans use *than* after the word *different*.

[8] **I could . . .** = It is possible for me to . . .

[9] **work out:** to exercise

[10] **without a doubt:** sure; of course

"I lift weights . . ."

He snaps his fingers.

It's a snap.[11] Tomorrow morning at ten o'clock.

In Richard and Marilyn's room the next morning. Richard is lifting weights. Marilyn is sewing.

Marilyn: Aren't you going to the aerobics class this morning?

Richard: *[He finishes exercising and puts the weights on the floor.]* Of course. Easy. *[He snaps his fingers.]* **No sweat.**[12]

Marilyn: You are not going to be able to move after this and the aerobics class.

Richard: Are you **kidding**[13] me? It's going to be **a piece of cake.**[14]

[Marilyn shakes her head no.]

Richard: **You want to bet?**[15]

Marilyn: Yeah. What's the **bet?**[16]

Richard: I bet **I can go**[17] one hour in your class this morning and not feel a thing!

Marilyn: The bet is—I win, and you cook dinner for the **entire**[18] family. Or you win, and I cook dinner for the entire family.

Richard: *[He shakes her hand.]* It's a bet.

Marilyn: OK. Call my instructor, Jack Davis, right now. His number is 555-8842. The advanced class starts at ten o'clock.

Richard: Well, it's eight twenty now.

Marilyn: It only takes eight minutes by bicycle to the aerobics class. Give him a call.

[Richard calls Jack Davis.]

[11] **It's a snap.** = [12]**No sweat.**
Both expressions mean "It's easy."

[13] **kidding:** joking with

[14] **a piece of cake:** easy

[15] **You want to bet?** = Do you want to bet?
bet *(verb)*: to agree to pay or do something, as in a game
In *Do you . . .* questions, it is common not to say *Do.* Also, Richard pronounces *want to* as *wanna.* This is a common informal pronunciation.

[16] **bet** *(noun)*: an agreement between two persons to pay or do something if one person is wrong

[17] **I can go . . .** = I can exercise . . .
Pronunciation: I *cn* go. When *can* has a verb after it, we do not usually pronounce the *a* in *can* because the word is not stressed. It is not a strong syllable in the sentence. (Here, *go* means "to exercise.")

[18] **entire:** whole

Jack: Davis Aerobics Center for Good Health.

Richard: Jack Davis, please.

Jack: This is Jack Davis.

Richard: Hello. This is Richard Stewart. My wife, Marilyn Stewart, is a member of your program. I'd like to come to the ten o'clock advanced class this morning.

Jack: Oh, fine, fine. Be here a few minutes early. You need to complete some forms before the class.

Richard: Thanks. I'm **on my way over.**[19]

Jack: Good-bye.

Richard: Bye-bye. *[He hangs up.]* It's all **set.**[20] I'm going. *[He puts his camera bag over his shoulder.]*

Marilyn: Bye.

Richard: See you later.

[They kiss.]

Marilyn: Good luck.

Richard: Don't forget about the bet. Dinner for the entire family. **And that includes Susan.**[21]

Marilyn: Don't *you* forget.

[Richard snaps his fingers and leaves. Marilyn snaps her fingers and smiles.]

END OF ACT I

[19] **on my way over:** leaving for a place

[20] **set:** arranged

[21] **And that includes Susan.**
Susan is Richard's sister. She doesn't live with the family. She has her own apartment in Manhattan.

U.S. LIFE

Aerobic exercises are very popular in the United States. Today, millions of Americans are exercising for good health. One out of every ten Americans exercises every day to stay **in shape** (in good physical condition). This **fitness craze** (interest in exercising and eating healthy foods) is popular all across the country.

Each year in many cities, including Boston, New York, San Fransisco, and Honolulu, there are long-distance races, or **marathons.** Even ordinary people run in these events. Every day in the United States, thousands of men, women, and children run through parks or city streets for good health.

More than ever before, a good diet and exercise program are important in the United States. Today, fitness is part of the American way of life.

☞ YOUR TURN

• What kinds of exercises are popular in your country?
• What exercises do you do every day?

ACT I

Activities

Here are some activities to help you check your understanding of Act I.

IDIOMS IN ACTION

Answer each of the following questions. Tell the truth about yourself. Circle *a, b,* or *c.*

1. Can you run a mile?
   a. Yes, it's a piece of cake.   **b.** Yes, but it's rough for me.   **c.** No, I can't.
2. Can you swim for half an hour without stopping?
   a. Yes, it's a snap.   **b.** Yes, but it's tough for me.   **c.** No, I can't.
3. Can you touch your toes without bending your knees?
   a. No problem.   **b.** Yes, but it's not easy for me.   **c.** No, I can't.
4. Can you lift thirty pounds?
   a. No sweat.   **b.** Yes, but it's difficult.   **c.** No, I can't.
5. Can you hold your breath for a minute?
   a. Yes, it's a piece of cake.   **b.** Yes, but it's hard.   **c.** No, I can't.

IN FACT

Reread Act I to find the answers to these questions. Write the answers on the lines. Try to find all the answers in two minutes!

1. How long does Richard lift weights every morning? _____
2. What time is the next aerobics class? _____
3. How long does Richard think he can exercise in the class? _____
4. What is Jack Davis's telephone number? _____
5. What time does Richard call Jack? _____
6. How long does it take to get to the class by bicycle? _____

THE BET

Marilyn and Richard make a bet about the aerobics class. Which *two* sentences explain their bet? Circle the numbers of the *two* correct answers.

1. Richard will be able to do aerobics with no problem, and Marilyn will cook dinner.
2. Richard will not be able to do aerobics, and Marilyn will cook dinner.
3. Marilyn will be able to do aerobics with no problem, and she will cook dinner.
4. Marilyn will not be able to do aerobics, and she will cook dinner.
5. Richard will not be able to do aerobics, and he will cook dinner.

ACT II

Outside, on a busy street in Riverdale. Inside, the Davis Aerobics Center for Good Health. Jack Davis is taking Richard's blood pressure.

Jack: OK, Richard. That's terrific. Your pressure is **120 over 75,**[1] and that's fine. Now stand up, please. *[Richard stands up, and Jack takes his blood pressure again.]* Good, it's **122 over 80.**[2] You can sit down now. When was your last complete physical?

Richard: *[He thinks.]* Six months ago.

Jack: Good. Do you have any back or knee problems?

Richard: **Nope.**[3] I am in perfect health.

Jack: **What do you do for a living,**[4] Mr. Stewart?

Richard: I'm a photographer.

Jack: Interesting. What do you photograph?

Richard: Everything. The American scene. People, places, events.

Jack: **Did you**[5] ever think of photographing an aerobics class?

Richard: No . . . I can't remember taking pictures of people exercising.

Jack: But **don't you**[6] think it'd be a good subject?

Richard: Sure.

Jack: I need some good photos for my advertising, Mr. Stewart. Maybe you can photograph a class, and I can give you and Mrs. Stewart a month of classes—free.

Richard: When can I photograph a class?

Jack: **Anytime.**[7]

Richard: How about today?

Jack: Terrific!

[1] **120 over 75;** [2] **122 over 80**
120 over 80 is perfect blood pressure.

[3] **Nope.** = No.
This is a very informal word.

[4] **What do you do for a living?** = What is your job?
A common pronunciation of *What do you* is *Waddaya.*

[5] **did you**
Jack uses the common informal pronunciation, *didja.*

[6] **don't you**
Jack uses the common informal pronunciation, *dontcha.*

[7] **Anytime.** = It's not important when; you decide.

U.S. LIFE

Many Americans have a **complete physical** once a year. During a complete physical, the doctor checks the patient's pulse and blood pressure. The patient may also have blood tests and a chest X-ray. At the end of a physical, the doctor may recommend a **fitness program** (a diet and exercise) for good health.

☞ YOUR TURN

When was your last complete physical?

In the exercise classroom at the Davis Aerobics Center. Jack Davis and another instructor are about to teach a class. Richard is taking many photographs.

"Stretch up . . ."

8 switch: change
9 twists: turns from side to side
10 tango: a dance from Argentina
11 ideal: perfect

Jack: *[He enters.]* Hi.

Instructor: Oh, hi.

Jack: Are we ready to go?

Instructor: Yeah. Yeah. *[to students]* Let's get in our lines. We're going to take it slow first. Stretch up . . . and we're going to go left first . . . 2, 3, 4 . . . now **switch.8** . . . OK, hold to the right. Sunrises. Stretch it out. Flat back. Bring it up . . . and **twists9** . . . and side . . . 2, 3 . . . and left . . . push . . . push . . . turn . . . hit the floor. Take it side again. . . . OK, and switch. Stretch it out. And we're going to warm down with a **tango.10** Left, right. Enjoy it.

In Richard and Marilyn's room later that day. Marilyn is alone, waiting for Richard. She is folding some towels. Richard sings and dances into the room.

Marilyn: Richard, did you go to the Davis Aerobics class today?

Richard: *[He takes off his camera and film bags and dances around the room.]* Yes, I went to the aerobics class today.

Marilyn: What is wrong with you?

Richard: Nothing. I am in excellent health. *[He starts dancing with Marilyn.]* I have **ideal11** blood pressure. A perfect heart. In other words, I'm in wonderful condition.

Marilyn: Richard, did you go to the aerobics class, really?

Richard: Don't forget to invite Susan for dinner.

Marilyn: *[not paying attention]* And your legs don't hurt?

Richard: *[He jumps up and down.]* Hurt? **What do you mean?**[12]

Marilyn: What about your arms? Lift your arms up like this. *[She lifts up her arms to show him, and he lifts his arms.]* And they don't hurt—not even a little?

Richard: Nope.

Marilyn: **You *are* in great condition.**[13] I can't believe it!

END OF ACT II

[12] **What do you mean?**
The informal pronunciation is *Waddayamean?*

[13] **You *are* in great condition.** = You *do* have a very strong and healthy body.

ACT II # *Activities*

Here are some activities to help you check your understanding of Act II.

PRONUNCIATION

Each of the following four sentences shows a typical pronunciation.
What is the correct spelling for each word or phrase in *italics*? Circle *a* or *b*.

1. *Waddaya* mean?
   a. What do you   **b.** What did you
2. *Didja* ever think of that?
   a. Did he   **b.** Did you
3. *Dontcha* like the idea?
   a. Don't you   **b.** Doesn't he
4. I *cn* do it.
   a. couldn't   **b.** can

WHAT'S THE ORDER?

Put the following sentences in the correct order. Rewrite them on the blank lines.

1. _____
2. _____
3. _____
4. _____

> The class begins.
> Richard goes home.
> Jack asks Richard to take photos of the class.
> Jack takes Richard's blood pressure.

AFTER CLASS

What happens after the class? Circle *a, b,* or *c*.

1. Richard sings and dances because
   a. he is happy that he won the bet, and he doesn't have to cook dinner for the entire family.
   b. he enjoys doing exercises, and he wants to teach some exercises to Marilyn.
   c. he wants Marilyn to think that he feels fine after exercising.
2. Richard makes Marilyn believe that
   a. he didn't really exercise.   **b.** he photographed the class.   **c.** he exercised with no problem.
3. Richard
   a. tells Marilyn the truth.   **b.** doesn't tell Marilyn the truth.   **c.** doesn't remember the truth.

QUESTIONS AND ANSWERS

Who asked each question, and who answered it? Fill in the blanks with the correct names and answers. Choose the answers to the questions from the box. The first one is done for you.

Anytime	Terrific	Nope

1. _____*Jack*_____ asked, "Do you have any back or knee problems?"
   _____*Richard*_____ answered, "_____*Nope*_____."
2. _____ asked, "When can I photograph a class?"
   _____ answered, "_____."
3. _____ asked, "How about today?"
   _____ answered, "_____."

Richard

Jack

ACT III

In the Stewarts' kitchen a little later. Richard is drinking a soda. Marilyn is writing a grocery list.

Marilyn: *[counting]* Grandpa, Ellen, Philip, Robbie, you and me. That's six steaks.

Richard: Don't forget Susan.

Marilyn: Seven steaks. Cooking dinner for the entire family is not so easy. *[She points to her list.]* The shopping: the salad: tomatoes, lettuce, cucumbers, and onions. The main course: steak and potatoes. Richard, **how much broccoli[1]** do I need for seven people?

Richard: Marilyn, I have to tell you something. At today's exercise class . . .

Marilyn: Yes, Richard.

Richard: Well, I didn't really exercise.

Marilyn: I knew it!

Richard: I wanted to, but Jack Davis needed a photographer. *[He laughs.]* I'm sorry, Marilyn.

Marilyn: I don't understand. Did you exercise or not?

Richard: No. Instead of exercising, I photographed the class.

Marilyn: And you didn't exercise?

Richard: No.

Marilyn: There's another advanced class today at four o'clock. We'll go together.

Richard: What about the bet?

Marilyn: Oh, the bet is still on, but *you* shop for the groceries. Remember, *you* win, and I cook dinner for the entire family.

Richard: You win, and *I* cook dinner for the entire family.

Marilyn: Including Susan. Four o'clock at the advanced exercise class. With me.

[They shake hands and laugh.]

Later, at the aerobics class. Marilyn and Richard are exercising to music. They are following the instructor's and Jack's directions.

Jack: Don't forget to breathe.

Instructor: Skip, hop, front. Twist . . . again. . . . OK, now . . . **scissors.[2]**

Richard: This is fun. It's a piece of cake.

Marilyn: Yeah. Just wait.

[1] How much broccoli . . . ?
We ask *how much* with uncountable nouns like *broccoli, lettuce, water,* and *traffic.* We ask *how many* with countable nouns like *tomatoes, onions, glasses,* and *cars.*

[2] scissors:

Here, the instructor means a kind of exercise.

"Skip, hop, front."

Instructor: 5, 6, 7, go right, 1, 2, back, 2, 3, 1, 2, 3, **pony,**[3] pony . . . 1, 2, 3, kick . . . 1, 2, 3, kick . . . pony. And twist, twist.

Jack: OK. Let's **pick up the pace.**[4]

[Richard is getting tired.]

Marilyn: How are you doing, Richard?

Richard: I can **barely**[5] move.

Instructor: 2, 3, 4, front. Now we're going to run it off. Front . . . knees up, knees up.

Jack: OK. Finish off by **jogging**[6] **in place.** [7] OK. Keep those knees up. All right. **That's it**[8] for today. Thank you, everyone. See you next week.

Richard: *[to Marilyn]* Thank you, Jack, but no thank you.

Marilyn: The advanced exercise class is not so easy, **huh?**[9]

[Richard slowly falls to the floor.]

Richard: No, no, you were right. I was wrong.

Marilyn: Come on, Richard. Get up. Let's go. You have to cook dinner for the entire family.

Richard: Marilyn, I'm exhausted. I can't move.

Marilyn: Oh, you'll do it. It's a piece of cake. *[She snaps her fingers.]*

Jack: Excuse me, Richard, Marilyn.

Richard: You are a terrific instructor, Jack.

Jack: Thanks. But I have a question. Is this your very first advanced aerobics class?

Richard: *[He laughs.]* Yes. It is.

Jack: You are **in great shape,**[10] Richard. Very few people **last**[11] in this class for the full hour the very first time.

Marilyn: It's true. You *are* in great shape.

Richard: Thanks!

Marilyn: I think we'll cook dinner together.

[They smile and kiss.]

END OF ACT III

[3] **pony:** a young horse
Here, the instructor means a dance step.

[4] **Pick up the pace.** = Move more quickly.

[5] **barely:** almost not at all

[6] **jogging:** running slowly for exercise

[7] **in place:** in the same position

[8] **That's it.** = That's the end.

[9] **Huh?** = Right?

[10] **in great shape:** in good physical condition
This is an informal use.

[11] **last:** can stay

ACT III

Activities

Here are some activities to help you check your understanding of this episode.

"HOW MUCH" AND "HOW MANY"

Marilyn asks, "Richard, how much broccoli do I need for seven people?"

> Use *how much* with uncountable nouns such as *water* and *rice*. Uncountable nouns do not usually appear in the plural form. Use *how many* with countable nouns such as *apples* and *oranges*.

Write **How much** or **How many** at the beginning of each of the following questions.

1. _____ tomatoes does she need?
2. _____ lettuce does she need?
3. _____ cucumbers does she need?
4. _____ onions does she need?
5. _____ salad does she need?
6. _____ potatoes does she need?
7. _____ steaks does she need?

WORD SEARCH

Read the clues. Then find the words and circle them. The answers are written across, down, or at an angle. Three answers are circled for you.

Clues

1. *Aerobics* are exercises for good breathing.
2. Jack *Davis*.
3. To exercise means the same as to *work* out.
4. A doctor's exam is a _____.
5. Jack offers a month of free _____ in his class.
6. Exercise and a diet are important for good _____.
7. Richard lifts _____.
8. Richard has a strong _____ in his arm.
9. It's easy! It's a piece of _____.
10. It's easy! It's a _____.
11. Richard jokes with Marilyn about being tired. He _____ her.
12. It's not a beginner's class; it's an _____ one.
13. Marilyn's husband's name is _____.
14. Richard and Marilyn make a _____ about the class.
15. Jack takes Richard's blood _____.
16. Richard shows Marilyn the muscle in his _____.

```
W A E R O B I C S L M P
E O D L E S S O N S B H
I B R V Q O Y C A K E Y
G A R K A U M B P R T S
H J R M E N T I R E D I
T E A S E S C D B X A C
S C D L P N E E Z K V A
S W R I C H A R D H I L
P R E S S U R E H O S K
E T O A J P M U S C L E
H E A L T H O J I T R M
```

EPISODE 5

"The Right Magic"

ACT I

In this episode, you will study . . .

VOCABULARY

cloudy	grateful
thrilled	patient
mild	emergency
well done	spoil

GRAMMAR AND EXPRESSIONS

making suggestions
negative *yes/no* questions
talking about the weather

ACT II

PRONUNCIATION

want to (wanna)
out of (outa)
the letters *ti (sh)*

  ### U.S. LIFE

- Do Americans have much leisure time?
- What are some typical superstitions in the United States?

☞ YOUR TURN

- What do you do in your leisure time?
- Do you have any superstitions?

ACT III

Here is the complete script with study material for Episode 5. Use these materials before *or* after you watch.

ACT I

In the Stewart's house early Saturday morning. Grandpa is making breakfast as Robbie enters.

Robbie: Hi, Grandpa.

Grandpa: Hi, Robbie.

Robbie: Can I help?

Grandpa: Yes, indeed. **Hand[1]** me two eggs from the **refrigerator,[2]** and I'll make you two **fried eggs.[3]**

Robbie: **How about[4]** some **bacon?[5]**

Grandpa: I made **enough for an army.[6] You going[7]** to the baseball game today? It's a perfect day for it—a little **cloudy[8]** but nice and warm.

Robbie: Dad and I were planning to go to the game, but he has to work today, and my friends don't **want to[9]** go. It's not an important game, **anyway.[10]**

Grandpa: Do you have any other plans for the day?

Robbie: I'll work on my computer. I have a new math **program,[11]** and I want to learn how to use it.

Grandpa: **Maybe you can[12]** teach me how to work on a computer someday.

Robbie: Anytime. It's really easy, but, like anything, you need to **work at it,[13]** Grandpa.

[They begin to eat breakfast.]

U.S. LIFE

Personal computers are very common in American homes today. These computers are used for education, business, and entertainment.

[1] **hand:** to give

[2] **refrigerator:**

[3] **fried eggs:**

[4] **How about . . . ?**
Use this phrase *to suggest* something.

[5] **bacon:**

[6] **enough for an army**
Use this expression to mean that you have *more than enough of* something. Of course, Grandpa didn't really cook enough bacon for an army.

[7] **You going . . . ?** = Are you going . . . ?
This is an informal use.

[8] **cloudy**
This is a *cloudy* sky:

[9] **want to**
Robbie uses the informal pronunciation, *wanna.*

[10] **anyway**
Use this word to show that you think something is not important. *Anyway* usually begins or ends a sentence.

[11] **program:** instructions on a disk to tell a computer what to do

[12] **Maybe you can . . .**
Use this phrase to suggest something for someone to do.

[13] **work at it:** to continue trying to do something

☞ **YOUR TURN**

Are personal computers popular in your country?

Robbie: *[eating]* This bacon is great. I love **crispy**[14] bacon.

Grandpa: Oh, **what are you doing tomorrow?**[15]

Robbie: **Nothing much.**[16]

Grandpa: Well, **maybe your dad and I could**[17] take you fishing with us.

Robbie: I'd like that, but . . .

Grandpa: But what?

Robbie: But Dad is always so busy.

Grandpa: Well, can you come fishing with me tomorrow?

Robbie: Sure, I can.

Later that morning. Philip is eating breakfast quickly. He is speaking with Grandpa.

Grandpa: Robbie says you can't take him to the game today.

Philip: I really feel bad about it, but they need me at the hospital today, in the **children's ward.**[18]

Grandpa: I understand.

Philip: Maybe we can spend some time together next weekend.

Grandpa: Definitely. We should. You and Robbie and me. Remember our first fishing trip?

Philip: I sure do . . . . Well, **I've got to run,**[19] Dad. See you later. *[He leaves.]*

On the patio later that day. Grandpa is looking at some fishing gear, things he will need for catching fish. Philip enters.

Philip: **Going fishing?**[20]

Grandpa: I'm thinking about it . . . . So, how's work?

Philip: Oh, the usual problems.

Grandpa: You're working pretty hard these days.

Philip: I guess I am.

Grandpa: When did you last go fishing with Robbie?

Philip: I remember exactly. It was on his birthday, June second, two years ago. *[He laughs.]* **We didn't catch anything.**[21]

[14] **crispy:** cooked so that it breaks easily

[15] **What are you doing tomorrow?** = What will you do tomorrow?
You can use the present progressive verb tense to refer to future plans.

[16] **Nothing much.** = Nothing important.

[17] **Maybe . . . could . . .**
You can use this phrase to make a suggestion.

[18] **children's ward:** the part of the hospital where children stay

[19] **I've got to run.** = I must leave right now.
This is an informal expression.

[20] **Going fishing?** = Are you going fishing?
Also use the verb *go* with these other activities:
go bowling, *go* running, *go* swimming, *go* dancing, and *go* shopping.

[21] **We didn't catch anything.** = We didn't get any fish.

Grandpa:	**Remember our fishing trips?**[22]
Philip:	Yes. I loved them.
Grandpa:	Remember catching your first fish?
Philip:	How can I forget? I fell **out of the boat!**[23] We had some good times together.
Grandpa:	Yes, we did. **Maybe we should**[24] do it again.
Philip:	How about tomorrow?
Grandpa:	**Don't you have to work?**[25]
Philip:	My **paper work**[26] will wait.
Grandpa:	Oh, Robbie will be **thrilled.**[27] I am, too, Son.
Philip:	I want to spend more time with Robbie.
Grandpa:	Tomorrow. **It'll be like old times**[28] for you and me. And Robbie will love it.
Philip:	Well, **what's the weather going to be like?**[29]
Grandpa:	**Radio says**[30] **sunny**[31] and **mild.**[32]
Philip:	Well, I'll tell Robbie. And thanks, Dad.
Grandpa:	Don't thank me. I'm just being a grandfather.

END OF ACT I

[22] **Remember our fishing trips?** = Do you remember our fishing trips?

[23] **out of the boat**
Philip says *outa the boat*. In informal conversation, people often do not pronounce the letter *f* in *of*.

[24] **Maybe . . . should . . .**
You can use this phrase to make a suggestion.

[25] **Don't you have to work?** = I thought you had to work.
Use a negative *yes/no* question if you thought something was true, but now you have a reason not to be sure. Before this conversation, Grandpa *thought* that Philip had to work tomorrow. But now Philip is suggesting a fishing trip, so Grandpa has a reason to believe that Philip *doesn't* have to work tomorrow.

[26] **paper work:** record keeping

[27] **thrilled:** excited and happy

[28] **It'll be like old times.**
You can use this expression about a future event that will be like a happy experience in the past.

[29] **What's the weather going to be like?**
Use this question to ask about the weather at a future time.

[30] **Radio says . . .** = The radio says . . .
Grandpa sometimes cuts the beginning of a sentence. Here, it is not correct to cut the article *the*.

[31] **sunny**
This is a *sunny* sky:

[32] **mild:** not too hot and not too cold

 U.S. LIFE

Like Philip, many Americans have trouble finding time for personal activities such as fishing. But most Americans are able to enjoy some **leisure time** each week. Because they are so busy, many Americans need to plan their leisure time carefully.

☞ **YOUR TURN**

• Do you have much leisure time?

• About how many hours of leisure time do you have each week?

ACT I

Activities

Here are some activities to help you check your understanding of Act I.

WEATHER

What's the weather going to be like in the U.S.A. today? Refer to the map to find your answers. Circle *a* or *b*.

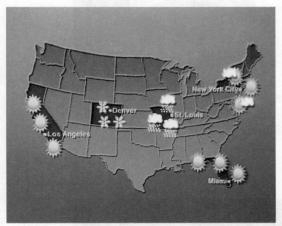

1. In New York City, it will be _____.
   a. sunny and a little cloudy   b. cloudy and raining
2. In Miami, it is going to be _____.
   a. cloudy and cold   **b.** sunny and hot
3. In St. Louis, you can expect _____.
   a. rain   b. snow
4. In Denver, it is going to _____.
   a. rain   **b.** snow
5. In Los Angeles, it'll be _____.
   a. sunny and a little cloudy   **b.** sunny and warm

FISHING FOR IDEAS

Whose ideas were these? Show the correct speaker for each of the sentences. Write the letter of each sentence inside a fish near the speaker's fishing line. One answer is given.

a. "Well, can you come fishing with me tomorrow?"

b. "Maybe we can spend some time together next weekend."

c. "Well, maybe your dad and I could take you fishing with us."

d. "I want to spend more time with Robbie."

e. "I'll work on my computer."

ACT II

At a lake in upstate New York the next morning. Grandpa, Philip, and Robbie are preparing to fish.

Robbie: This is really neat! When do we eat?

Philip: First, we have to catch some fish. In order to catch fish, you have to do this. *[He prepares the fishing line.]* **Here we go.**[1] That's it. Then drop it into the water. All of this comes **before eating.**[2] OK?

Robbie: How do you know so much about fishing?

Philip: Grandpa taught me. We spent a lot of time fishing together. **Now, the important thing is to get the hook close to the fish.**[3] All right? Like this. *[He puts his fishing line into the water.]*

Robbie: I think I see some fish right under us, Dad.

Philip: Oh, **not a chance!**[4]

Robbie: I just saw a big one!

[A young boy arrives with a fishing rod.]

Grandpa: **Hi, there!**[5]

Albert: Hi.

Grandpa: What's your name?

Albert: Albert.

Grandpa: Are you **all**[6] alone?

Albert: Yes, sir.

Grandpa: How old are you, Albert?

Albert: I'm ten.

Philip: Where's your father?

Albert: He's up there at the **lodge.**[7]

Philip: Does he know you're here?

Albert: Yes, sir.

Philip: OK, Robbie, maybe you should watch him. The water's pretty deep here.

Robbie: I'll watch him, Dad.

A little while later. They are still fishing.

Robbie: What time is it?

Grandpa: It's almost lunchtime, and no fish yet.

Robbie: I can go up to the lodge for some hot dogs and drinks.

Philip: **No way!**[8] We're here to catch our lunch.

[1] **Here we go.** = We're starting now. This is an informal expression.

[2] **before eating**
Use an *-ing* verb form *(eating)* after a preposition *(before)*.

[3] **Now, the important thing is to get the hook close to the fish.**
Philip is trying to be funny. Of course Robbie knows that the hook must be near the fish.

hook

[4] **Not a chance!** = That's impossible.

[5] **Hi, there!**
This is an informal way to say *hello.*

[6] **all:** completely

[7] **lodge:** a small house to stay in during a trip or vacation

[8] **No way!** = Absolutely not; forget it.

Grandpa:	To catch fish, you need the right magic.
Philip:	That's right. I forgot! The right magic. Do it for Robbie, Dad.
Grandpa:	You remember?
Philip:	Sure. **Come on.**[9]
Grandpa:	Well, first, you have to turn your hat around like this. Then you close your eyes and say the magic words. Fish, fish, send me a fish.
Robbie:	*[He closes his eyes.]* Fish, fish, send me a fish . . . . I got one!
Grandpa:	See, it works!
Robbie:	It's a big one!
Philip:	Well, it always worked for me, too.
Robbie:	Grandpa, get the **net,**[10] please!

[Grandpa gets the net, and Robbie finally catches the fish.]

Robbie:	Dad, you got one, too!
Philip:	**You bet**[11] I have! *[Philip brings up a boot from the water.]*
Grandpa:	Easy, Philip, easy.
Robbie:	Sorry, Dad.
Philip:	Well, one more and I've got a pair of boots.
Robbie:	You didn't say the magic words.
Grandpa:	Robbie's right.
Philip:	Yes, but *you* did, and we've got our lunch. **Let's**[12] build a fire and cook it! Come on, Albert, you can help us!
Albert:	I want to stay here and fish.
Grandpa:	All right, but be careful.

9 Come on. = Do it now.

10 net:

11 You bet. = You can be sure.

12 Let's . . . = Let us . . .
Use *Let's* to make a suggestion for you and someone else to do something.

 **U.S. LIFE**

Grandpa tells Robbie that to catch fish, he should say, "Fish, fish, send me a fish." For Grandpa, this is "the right magic." It is his own **superstition**. To have a superstition is to believe that something brings good or bad luck, with no scientific reason to think so. There are many common good-luck superstitions in the U.S. Finding a four-leaf clover and knocking on wood are two examples. Some people believe that walking under a ladder and the number 13 bring bad luck. In many apartment and office buildings in the U.S., there is no 13th floor. The 14th floor follows the 12th!

a four-leaf clover

☞ **YOUR TURN**

• What are some common superstitions in your country?
• Do you have any superstitions of your own? If so, what are they?

A little later. Grandpa, Philip, and Robbie are around their campfire.

Robbie: Is it finished yet?
Philip: I think so. I hope you like your fish **well done.**[13]
Grandpa: **Burned,**[14] you mean.
Philip: Hey, I'm a doctor, not a **chef.**[15]

[They hear Albert calling from the lake.]

Albert: Help! Help! I can't swim!
Robbie: Dad! Grandpa! He fell in!

[Robbie and Philip rush to save Albert. They pull him from the water and place him on the dock.]

Philip: **Easy does it,**[16] Robbie. **That a boy.**[17] **That's it.**[18]
Grandpa: He's not breathing, Philip!
Philip: Robbie, run to the car! Bring a **blanket**[19] and my medical bag.
Robbie: Yes, Dad.

[Philip slowly breathes into the boy's mouth.]

Philip: Now, come on, **son.**[20] Come on, son.
Grandpa: Breathe, Albert!

END OF ACT II

[13] **well done:** cooked for a long time
[14] **burned:** cooked too long
[15] **chef:** a professional cook

[16] **Easy does it.** = Relax; go slowly.
[17] **That a boy.** = [18] **That's it.**
These two expression mean "You're doing well."
[19] **blanket**
When you go to sleep, you cover yourself with a *blanket*.

[20] **son**
Of course, Albert isn't really Philip's son. Older people sometimes use *son* to speak directly to a young boy.

ACT II ▶ *Activities*

Here are some activities to help you check your understanding of Act II.

DESCRIBING A SEQUENCE

What was the correct sequence of events in Act II? Complete each sentence in the following paragraph. For each answer, use a phrase that is under one of the pictures.

First, Grandpa, Philip, and Robbie _arrived at the lake_ .

Next, Grandpa _used the right magic_. **After that,** Robbie _caught a fish_ .

Later on, they _cooked the fish_ . **Finally,** Albert _fell in the water_ .

caught a fish

used the right magic

fell in the water

cooked the fish

arrived at the lake

CATCH PHRASES [freiz]

Here are some lines of dialogue from Act II. Which line came after each of the following sentences? Choose the correct answer from the fishing net. Then write the answer on the blank line.

1. Robbie: I can go up to the lodge for some hot dogs and drinks.
   Philip: _no way_

2. Philip: The right magic. Do it for Robbie, Dad.
   Grandpa: You remember?
   Philip: _sure come on_

3. Robbie: Dad, you got one, too!
   Philip: _you bet I have_

4. Philip: I hope you like your fish well done.
   Grandpa: _burned you mean_

Burned, you mean
You bet I have!
No way!
Sure. Come on.

ACT III

A few minutes later. Robbie returns with Philip's medical bag. Philip is trying to save the boy's life.

Robbie: Here's the bag. Will he be OK, Dad?

Philip: I hope so. *[to Albert]* That's it. That's the way. That's it. There. Oh, it's going to be all right. That's it. *[to Grandpa]* **Wrap**[1] him in the blanket, Dad! *[to Albert]* That's it. That's it. It's all right, Albert. You're going to be OK.

Albert: I want my daddy!

Philip: We'll take you to him. Easy now. Easy does it. That's it.

Outside the lodge a little later.

Grandpa: Your dad is **quite a guy.**[2]

Robbie: I know, Grandpa.

[Philip comes out of the lodge. Albert's father is with him.]

Grandpa: How is he, Philip?

Philip: He's asleep. He's going to be fine.

Father: How can I thank all of you?

Philip: Thank my son Robbie. He pulled him out of the water.

Father: I'm very **grateful,**[3] Robbie.

Robbie: Dad saved him, not me.

Father: I'm so thankful to all of you. *[He shakes their hands and leaves.]*

Philip: **So long.**[4]

Grandpa: He's a lucky boy. Well, **what do you say we**[5] get back to our fishing?

Philip: That's a great idea. *[His **beeper**[6] sounds.]* **Uh-oh.**[7] It's probably the hospital. I have to **get to**[8] a phone. It probably means we can't stay.

Robbie: That's OK.

[Philip goes into the lodge to telephone the hospital. A few minutes later, he returns.]

Philip: One of may **patients**[9] has a high fever, and I have to go to the hospital. I'm sorry, Robbie. I guess I ruined your day.

Robbie: You didn't ruin my day, Dad. I understand. I really do.

In the Stewarts' kitchen later that day. Ellen is cooking. Grandpa and Robbie enter.

Ellen: **Why are you back**[10] so early?

Grandpa: Philip had to go back to the hospital.

[1] **wrap:** to fold around; cover

[2] **quite a guy:** a wonderful man

[3] **grateful:** thankful

[4] **So long.** = Good-bye.

[5] **What do you say we . . . ?**
Use this phrase to make an informal suggestion.

[6] **beeper**
A doctor often carries a *beeper* so that a hospital can call him. The beeper makes a sound, and then the doctor knows that he should call the hospital.

[7] **Uh-oh.**
This sound shows that there is a problem.

[8] **get to:** to go to immediately

[9] **patients**
A *patient* is a sick person. Doctors take care of patients, often in a hospital.
In this word, the letters *ti* sound like *sh*. Other examples include words ending in *-tion*, such as *nation* and *election*.

[10] **Why are you back . . . ?** = Why did you return . . . ?

Robbie:	He had an **emergency.**[11]
Ellen:	Oh, that's too bad, Robbie. Did it **spoil**[12] your fun?
Robbie:	No, Mom. We had a great time.
Ellen:	Well, did you do any fishing?
Robbie:	Yeah, we caught lots of them. Look! *[He empties a bag onto the table.]* They had a special on **frozen fish**[13] down at the supermarket.
Ellen:	*[She lifts the bag.]* Oh, you really had a bad day.
Grandpa:	We had a good day. Robbie pulled a boy out of the water.
Robbie:	And Dad saved his life. He's a terrific doctor, Mom.
Ellen:	I know.

In the Stewarts' kitchen that night. Grandpa and Robbie are doing the dishes.

Philip:	*[He enters.]* Hi, **Pop.**[14] Hi, Son.
Robbie:	Hello, Dad.
Philip:	What a day!
Grandpa:	How about a cup of coffee, Son?
Philip:	I'd love a cup of coffee.
Robbie:	How was the patient?
Philip:	She'll be fine.
Robbie:	Was it serious?
Philip:	No.
Robbie:	Until today, I was never really interested in medicine.
Philip:	Well, it's hard work.
Robbie:	Now I know.
Philip:	*[He pats Robbie on the back.]* I had a good time today, Robbie.
Robbie:	Me, too.
Philip:	**Why don't we**[15] do it again?
Robbie:	Can we? When?
Philip:	How about next Saturday?
Robbie:	Won't you be busy?
Philip:	I'm changing my **schedule.**[16] Well, do we have a date?
Robbie:	We sure do, Dad. Grandpa, can you come?
Grandpa:	I have other plans, Robbie. But I think you two can have a good time together without me.
Philip:	No, Dad, and certainly not without the right magic.

END OF ACT III

[11] **emergency:** a sudden situation that needs fast action

[12] **spoil:** to ruin

[13] **frozen fish:**

[14] **Pop:** Dad; Father

[15] **Why don't we . . . ?**
You can use this phrase to begin a suggestion.

[16] **schedule:** a list of the times for certain things to happen

ACT III Activities

Here are some activities to help you check your understanding of this episode.

MAKING SUGGESTIONS

There are many ways to begin a suggestion in English. Grandpa and Philip use the following phrases to make suggestions in this episode.

Maybe . . . could	Maybe . . . can	Maybe . . . should	
What do you say	Why don't	How about	Let's

How did Grandpa and Philip make each of the suggestions below?
Look back at the script to find the correct words to complete each blank space.

ACT I

1. Grandpa: Well, ___may be___ your dad and I ___could___ take you fishing with us.
2. Philip: ___maybe___ we ___scan___ spend some time together next weekend.
3. Grandpa: ___may be___ we ___should___ do it again.
4. Philip: ___How about___ tomorrow?

ACT II

5. Philip: OK, Robbie, ___May be___ you ___should___ watch him.
6. Philip: ___Let's___ build a fire and cook it.

ACT III

7. Grandpa: Well, ___What Do you say___ we get back to our fishing?
8. Philip: ___why don't___ we do it again?
9. Philip: ___How about___ next Saturday?

WHAT DO YOU SAY?

What can you say in each of the following situations? Choose the best sentence or phrase from the box. Then write it on the blank line.

I'm very grateful	It'll be like old times	I'm thrilled	I've got to run
Nothing much	Come on	You bet	

1. You must stop talking to your friend because you are late for an appointment. You say, "___I've got to run___."
2. You were feeling sad. Then a friend talked to you for many hours. Now you are feeling much better. You want to thank your friend, so you say, "___I'm very grateful___."
3. You are in love for the first time in your life. Someone asks you, "How do you feel?" You say, "___I'm thrilled___."
4. Your friend is afraid to tell you his problem. You want to help him, so you say, "___Come on___. You can talk to me."
5. You have no special plans for next weekend. A friend asks, "What are you doing next Saturday?" You answer, "___nothing much___."
6. You receive a surprise telephone call from an old friend. You last spoke to her ten years ago. You plan to meet for dinner tomorrow. You say, "___it'll be like old time___"
7. A friend asks you to help her, and you want to help. She asks, "Are you sure you have enough time?" You answer, "___You bet___!"

EPISODE 6

"Thanksgiving"

ACT I

ACT II

ACT III

In this episode, you will study . . .

VOCABULARY

ingredient	band	settler
grouchy	clown	harvest
parade	recipe	touchdown

GRAMMAR AND EXPRESSIONS

expressing possibilities
any in negative sentences
come by
What's gotten into (someone)?
get over
look forward to
go along with

PRONUNCIATION

the letter *c* (*s* and *k* sounds)
sounds to show surprise

 ### U.S. LIFE

• How do Americans celebrate the Thanksgiving holiday?
• What is the history of this holiday?

☞ YOUR TURN

What is your favorite holiday?

Here is the complete script with study material for Episode 6. Use these materials before *or* after you watch.

ACT I

In the kitchen in the Stewarts' home on Thanksgiving morning. Philip is drinking coffee.

Ellen: OK, Philip. This is your third cup of coffee. We should **get to work,**[1] or we won't be finished by dinnertime.

Philip: I guess we must.

Ellen: We *must.*

Philip: OK. *[He walks to the table in the center of the room.]* The beginning of my famous Thanksgiving apple pie. *[He picks up an apple.]* One apple. Two apples. Three apples. Four apples.

Ellen: Come on, Philip! Get busy with your famous apple pie. **There's much more to be done.**[2]

Philip: *[thinking]* Now, the **ingredients.**[3]

Philip: What goes into my apple pie besides apples? Ah, yes. Flour, sugar, butter. *[He looks in the refrigerator and carries the butter dish to the table.]* Butter, nice and cold and hard. OK, here are the **walnuts.**[4] Last but not least, the reason my apple pie is famous—**cinnamon.**[5] Cinnamon . . . *[He begins to look for the cinnamon.]* Ellen, where's the cinnamon?

Ellen: If there is any cinnamon, it's in the **cabinet**[6] with the salt and pepper.

Philip: *[He opens the cabinet. He brings the spice rack to the table.]* Salt, pepper, dill weed, garlic powder, cinnamon. Ellen?

Ellen: Yes, Philip.

Philip: Is it possible that we forgot to buy cinnamon?

Ellen: Yes, **it is possible that**[7] we forgot to buy cinnamon.

Philip: Well, how can I make my famous apple pie without cinnamon?

---

[1] **get to work:** to start to work

[2] **There's much more to be done.** = We have a lot more to do.

[3] **ingredients:** the things you mix together to prepare a food

[4] **walnuts:**

[5] **cinnamon:** a kind of spice
A *spice* is a material from a plant. We use spices to give flavor to food.
The letter *c* sounds like *s* in this word. The letter *c* usually sounds like *s* before *i, e,* and *y.* Otherwise, it sounds like *k.*

spice rack

[6] **cabinet:** a place to keep things such as dishes and food

[7] **It is possible that . . .** = Maybe . . .

U.S. LIFE

Thanksgiving is a happy holiday on the fourth Thursday of each November. Americans of all religions celebrate this holiday with big dinners and family reunions. It is a time to remember all the good things in life and to be thankful.

☞ YOUR TURN

- In your country, is there a special holiday for feeling thankful?
- What is your favorite holiday?

[Robbie enters.]

Robbie:	Good morning.
Ellen:	Oh, hi, Robbie. Good morning.
Philip:	Good morning, Robbie. **Can you do me a favor?**[8]
Robbie:	Sure, Dad. What?
Philip:	Remember my apple pie on Thanksgiving? What do you *love* about it?
Robbie:	The apples?

Philip:	No. The *sssss* . . .
Robbie:	Cinnamon!
Philip:	Right. **We don't have any**[9] cinnamon.
Robbie:	I'll go down to Henry's grocery. He's alway open. I'll get some for you.
Philip:	**That's my boy!**[10] [He takes money from his pocket and hands it to Robbie.]
Ellen:	Oh, put your heavy jacket on, Robbie. It's cold outside.
Robbie:	**Alexandra might call.**[11] Tell her I'll **call her right back.**[12]
Ellen:	OK.
Philip:	Thanks, Son.

[Robbie leaves.]

Ellen:	Uh, why does he always have to **slam the door?**[13]

A little later. The telephone rings in the kitchen. Ellen answers it.

Ellen:	Hello. . . . Hello, Alexandra. How are you? . . . Fine. Robbie just went to the store. He'll be back soon. He said he'll call you. . . . Oh, oh, **I see.**[14] . . . Oh . . . certainly. Well, do you have the phone number there? . . . Oh . . . I see. . . . Please, I know he wants to talk to you. . . . Thank you, and happy Thanksgiving to you and your family, too. Try to **come by**[15] later for dessert. . . . Bye.

[8] **Can you do me a favor?** = Can you do something for me?

[9] **We don't have any . . .** = We have no . . .
A negative sentence with *any* usually means the same as a positive sentence with *no*.

[10] **That's my boy!** = You're a good son.

[11] **Alexandra might call.** = Maybe Alexandra will call, *or* Alexandra may call.

[12] **call her right back:** to telephone her immediately

[13] **slam the door** = to close the door with force, making a loud noise

[14] **I see.** = I understand.

[15] **come by:** to visit for a short time

Ellen:	*[to Philip]* That was Alexandra. She and the Molinas are going to spend Thanksgiving with their cousins. She doesn't have the phone number.
Philip:	Oh, Robbie will be disappointed.
Ellen:	He'll be **grouchy.**[16] Maybe she'll call back. She promised.
Robbie:	*[He returns from the store.]* Here's your cinnamon, Pop. It was a dollar and sixty cents. You forgot to ask me for the **change.**[17]
Philip:	Or did you forget to give it to me?

[Robbie gives him the change. Philip puts it in his pocket.]

Philip:	Thanks, Son.
Ellen:	Alexandra called.
Robbie:	I'll call her back.
Ellen:	She said she'll call you later. She's not at home.

[Robbie dials Alexandra's telephone number anyway. She doesn't answer.]

Philip:	You *should* have your breakfast, Son. **Make you feel better.**[18] **Protein,**[19] vitamins.
Robbie:	She said *she'll* call back?
Ellen:	Yes, she did.
Grandpa:	*[He enters the kitchen.]* Good morning, everyone! Happy Turkey Day! What's wrong?
Robbie:	Nothing. *[angry]* Absolutely nothing. *[He leaves the room.]*
Grandpa:	**What's gotten into him?**[20]
Ellen:	He missed a phone call.
Grandpa:	From . . .?
Philip:	Yes, Alexandra.
Grandpa:	It's nice to see young love. . . . Oh, to be young again! Where's the coffee?

END OF ACT I

[16] **grouchy:** in a bad mood; complaining

[17] **change:** the money returned to you after you pay for something
If Robbie gave the grocer five dollars, and the cinnamon cost a dollar and sixty cents, Robbie's *change* was three dollars and forty cents.

[18] **Make you feel better.** = It will make you feel better.

[19] **protein**
Eating foods with *protein* is necessary for a healthy diet. Meat, cheese, eggs, and fish contain protein.

[20] **What's gotten into him?** = What's bothering him?

 ## U.S. LIFE

Grandpa says, "Happy Turkey Day!" because turkey is a traditional Thanksgiving Day food.

☞ **YOUR TURN**

What foods are typical on different holidays in your country?

ACT I *Activities*

Here are some activities to help you check your understanding of Act I.

POSSIBILITIES

Here are some possibilities. Rewrite each sentence. Use the word in parentheses. The first answer is given.

1. It's possible that Alexandra will call again
   (*might*) **Alexandra might call again.**
2. It's possible that Philip will have another cup of coffee.
   (*may*) _____
3. It's possible that Robbie will feel better soon.
   (*maybe*) _____
4. It's possible that Grandpa will talk to Robbie.
   (*might*) _____
5. It's possible that Alexandra will come by for dessert.
   (*maybe*) _____

SPECIAL INGREDIENTS

Philip names six ingredients for his "famous Thanksgiving apple pie." List as many ingredients as you can remember. Then look back at the script to check your answers.

1. _____
2. _____
3. _____
4. _____
5. _____
6. _____

THANKSGIVING MORNING

Here are some of the events at the Stewarts' home on Thanksgiving morning. Show the correct order by numbering the events from 1–8. One answer is given.

____ **a.** Alexandra called.
____ **b.** Robbie went to the store.
____ **c.** Philip looked for the cinnamon.
____ **d.** Grandpa came into the kitchen.
_1_ **e.** Philip counted the apples for his apple pie.
____ **f.** Philip gave Robbie some money.
____ **g.** Robbie gave Philip the change.
____ **h.** Robbie tried to telephone Alexandra.

ACT II

In the Stewarts' living room later that day. Grandpa and Robbie are watching the Thanksgiving Day parade on television.

Grandpa: I love **parades.**[1] The Thanksgiving Day parade is always such great fun. *[He points to the TV screen.]* Look at that Superman **balloon!**[2] **Wowee!**[3] Just floating along high above Central Park West. Don't you just love it? Oh, and the **bands**[4] and the music. John Philip Sousa. I love his music. *[He sings with the music from the television.]* Da dada da da dada da da da da da da dada. Oh, look at that **float,**[5] Robbie. Look at those funny-looking **clowns.**[6]

Robbie: It's for kids.

Grandpa: **Maybe so,**[7] but parades always make me feel like a kid. Remember when you and your dad and I went to the Thanksgiving Day parade? You were four or five years old, I think.

[The telephone rings in the kitchen. Robbie rushes to answer it.]

U.S. LIFE

Every Thanksgiving, Macy's department store organizes a parade in New York City. In the parade, there are large floats, balloons of popular cartoon characters, famous television stars, and bands from all over the United States. These bands often play the music of John Philip Sousa, a famous American composer. He wrote more than a hundred marches. The Thanksgiving Day Parade begins on Central Park West, a street on the west side of Manhattan. Each year, more than 55 million people watch this parade on television. Many other large American cities also have Thanksgiving Day parades. Macy's started this tradition in 1924.

[1] parades:

a parade

[2] balloon:

[3] Wowee!
You can say *Wow!* or *Wowee!* when you are surprised or excited. *Wowee!* is usually a child's expression. Both sounds are informal.

[4] bands:

a band

[5] float:

[6] clowns:

[7] Maybe so. = Maybe that's true.

☞ YOUR TURN

When can you see parades in your country?

Robbie:	Hello, hello. . . . Oh, hi, Susan. How are you? . . . Here's Mom. *[He hands the phone to Ellen and returns to the living room.]*
Ellen:	Hello, Susan. Yes, he missed a phone call from Alexandra. Yes, I know, but he'll **get over it.**[8] Good. Then you'll be here about five? Oh, fine. I **look forward to**[9] seeing you and Harry and Michelle. Drive carefully. Good-bye.
Philip:	*[He enters the living room with a bowl.]* Taste Ellen's **turkey dressing.**[10] It's delicious.
Grandpa:	I'm not surprised. It's Grandma's **recipe.**[11]
Robbie:	It's my favorite part of the meal.
Philip:	What about my famous apple pie?
Robbie:	Dad, your apple pie is my favorite dessert.
Philip:	How's the parade?
Robbie:	OK.

[The phone rings again.]

Robbie:	*[calling]* Mom! Is it for me?
Ellen:	No, Robbie.
Philip:	Who was it?
Ellen:	*[She comes into the living room.]* **Wrong number.**[12] Philip, would you join me in the kitchen, please? It's getting late. We have vegetables to prepare.
Robbie:	Can I help with anything?
Ellen:	No, honey. You just relax with Grandpa. I'll get you **to help serve**[13] later. *[She and Philip leave the living room.]*
Grandpa:	Ellen reminds me so much of Grandma.
Philip:	*[He returns to the living room.]* What time does the **Michigan**[14] football game **come on?**[15]
Robbie:	Four.
Ellen:	*[calling from the kitchen]* Philip!
Philip:	I'll be back to see the game. *[He returns to the kitchen.]*
Robbie:	Grandpa, when did Dad graduate from Michigan?
Grandpa:	Let me think. He graduated from medical school in 1960 and from the University of Michigan in 1956.
Robbie:	Did you go to Michigan, too, Grandpa?
Grandpa:	**Yup.**[16] I graduated in 1937.
Robbie:	**I've got to**[17] start thinking about college soon.

[The phone rings again. Robbie runs to answer it.]

END OF ACT II

[8] **get over it:** to stop feeling bad about it

[9] **look forward to:** to wait for with pleasure
A verb following this expression is always in the *-ing* form.

[10] **turkey dressing:** pieces of bread with spices, often cooked inside the turkey.
This kind of *dressing* is sometimes called *stuffing*.

[11] **recipe:** directions for preparing food

[12] **Wrong number.** = Someone called the wrong telephone number.

[13] **to help serve:** to help to serve
After the verb *help*, the word *to* is not necessary before another verb.

[14] **Michigan:** the University of Michigan
The University of Michigan is a large university in the state of Michigan.

[15] **come on:** to begin
Use *come on* with this meaning only to refer to television or radio programs.

[16] **Yup.** = Yes.
This is an informal way to say *yes*.

[17] **I've got to . . .** = I have got to . . . *or* I have to . . .
This expression means "I must."

U.S. LIFE

Watching college football games on television is a typical Thanksgiving Day activity.

☞ YOUR TURN

Which sports are popular in your country?

ACT II *Activities*

Here are some activities to help you check your understanding of Act II.

LIKES AND DISLIKES

Complete each sentence with the correct answer. For each sentence, choice *a* is an expression of *like*; choice *b* is an expression of *dislike*. Circle *a* or *b*.

1. At the beginning of Act II, Grandpa _____ watching the Thanksgiving Day parade.
   a. loves   **b.** doesn't enjoy
2. At the beginning of Act II, Robbie _____ watching the Thanksgiving Day parade.
   a. loves   **b.** doesn't enjoy
3. Philip really _____ Ellen's turkey dressing.
   a. likes   **b.** doesn't like
4. Philip _____ football.
   a. is crazy about   **b.** doesn't like
5. Ellen _____ it when Robbie slams the door.
   a. loves   **b.** can't stand
6. Robbie _____ waiting for Alexandra to call.
   a. is fond of   **b.** hates

WHAT AND WHO

A. What is the reference of the underlined pronoun in each item? Choose the answers from Box A. Write the letter of each correct answer on the line next to each sentence.

1. Robbie: It's for kids. ____
2. Ellen: . . . he'll get over it. ____
3. Grandpa: It's Grandma's recipe. ____
4. Robbie: Is it for me? ____

A
a. missing the telephone call
b. the telephone call
c. the parade
d. Ellen's turkey dressing

B. What is the reference of the underlined pronoun in each item? Choose the answers from Box B. Write the letter of each correct answer on the line next to each sentence.

1. Grandpa: . . . parades always make me feel like a kid. ____
2. Ellen: . . . he missed a phone call from Alexandra. ____
3. Ellen: I look forward to seeing you and Harry and Michelle. ____
4. Ellen: . . . would you join me in the kitchen, please? ____

B
a. Philip
b. Grandpa
c. Susan
d. Robbie

ACT III

Later that afternoon. The Stewart family and Harry and Michelle are sitting around the table. They are ready to have their Thanksgiving Day dinner.

Philip: OK, everybody. I want to welcome Harry and his daughter Michelle to Thanksgiving with us.

Harry: Thank you, Dr. Stewart.

Philip: Call me Philip.

Harry: OK.

Philip: But first, I think we should take a moment and remember the meaning of Thanksgiving.

Harry: Philip, I took Michelle to a school play about the first Thanksgiving.

Philip: Well, why don't you tell us about that, Michelle?

Michelle: Thanksgiving was about the Pilgrims, the first **settlers**[1] in America. They shared the first **harvest**[2] with the Indians and gave thanks.

Philip: All right. Then **in that spirit**[3] let's each of us **give thanks.**[4] Each in his own way. Who wants to begin?

Grandpa: I will. I give thanks for being here with my family and for being well, so I can enjoy you all.

Robbie: All right! We love you, Grandpa.

Susan: I'd like to give thanks for a healthy year, a good job, and for meeting Harry and Michelle.

Harry: We'd like to give thanks for meeting Susan and the Stewart family.

Michelle: I love you, Daddy.

Susan: *[speaking softly to Harry]* Thanks, Harry. **That was very kind of you.**[5]

Robbie: I'd like to give thanks for Grandpa coming to live with us. And I'd also like to thank my math teacher for giving me a passing grade. And *[with hope]* call me, Alexandra.

Ellen: Oh, Robbie!

Grandpa: She'll call.

Richard: You go first, Marilyn.

Marilyn: I'm thinking. You go first.

Richard: Well, you all know I'm working on my photo album. It's not finished yet. *[He looks at Marilyn.]* And I'd like to thank Marilyn for being so **patient.**[6]

[1] **settlers:** people who come to live in a new place

[2] **harvest:** the grains, fruit, and vegetables of the season

[3] **in that spirit:** with the same kind of feeling

[4] **give thanks:** to say thank you

[5] **That was very kind of you.**
You can use this expression to thank someone.

[6] **patient:** calm and not complaining

U.S. LIFE

The **Pilgrims** were a group of English settlers who came to Massachusetts in 1620. They came to America because they wanted religious freedom. They arrived at Plymouth, Massachusetts, on a ship called the *Mayflower*. Their first winter was difficult, and many of the Pilgrims died. But the following year, the corn harvest was good, and there was a celebration for three days. That was the first Thanksgiving.

☞ YOUR TURN

Is there a special holiday to celebrate the harvest in your country?

Marilyn: Thanks, Richard. I should thank *you* for **encouraging**[7] me to keep working on my fashion designs. I'm lucky to have a husband **with an artistic eye.**[8]

Ellen: Oh, we have a lot to be thankful for. For the food on this table. Just like the Pilgrims.

Philip: I'll **go along with**[9] that, Ellen.

Ellen: Well, help me serve, Robbie.

[They begin to serve the dinner.]

Later, after dinner.

Harry: It was a wonderful meal, Mrs. Stewart. Thank you.

Richard: And now to see the end of the football game.

Philip: Exactly. *[He gets up.]*

Ellen: Where are you going, Philip?

Philip: Remember, the Michigan football game? And Michigan needs a **touchdown.**[10]

Ellen: Did you forget something?

Robbie: Dad, your famous apple pie.

Philip: Just let me see the score, Ellen.

Marilyn: Go ahead, Philip. We should all **take a little break**[11] before dessert.

[Philip and Richard go into the living room. The other members of the family take the dishes from the table. Then the doorbell rings.]

Ellen: Oh, who **could**[12] that be? Oh, it must be Alexandra. I invited her to come by for dessert.

Robbie: You did?

[Ellen and Robbie go to the the front door.]

Grandpa: I like Ellen.

[Alexandra enters.]

Robbie: You know everyone, Alexandra.

Ellen: No, she doesn't know Harry Bennett and his daughter Michelle.

Alexandra: Nice to meet you.

Harry &
  Michelle: Hi.

Marilyn &
  Susan: Hello, Alexandra.

Alexandra: Hi, Marilyn. Hi, Susan. Happy Thanksgiving.

Ellen: And Alexandra brought us a **pumpkin pie.**[13]

[7] **encouraging:** giving courage, hope, or confidence

[8] **with an artistic eye:** able to see things as an artist

[9] **go along with:** to agree with

[10] **touchdown**
In football, you score six points by catching the ball or running with it across the other team's goal line.

[11] **take a little break:** to rest for a short time

[12] **could:** might

[13] **pumpkin pie:**

pumpkins   pumpkin pie

Robbie: Please sit down, Alexandra. *[calling]* Dad, Richard—Alexandra's here.

[Richard and Philip come into the kitchen.]

Richard: Michigan needs a touchdown. Three minutes to play. Hi, Alexandra. Welcome.

Philip: Hello, Alexandra. Yes, Michigan needs a touchdown. One tiny little touchdown, with just three minutes to play.

Alexandra: You want Michigan to win.

Philip: **How'd¹⁴** you guess?

Ellen: And Alexandra brought us a *pumpkin* pie.

[Philip walks to the oven. He turns around with a strange look on his face.]

Ellen: What happened?

Philip: We forgot to turn the oven on.

Ellen: *We* did? Philip, why don't you go watch the last three minutes of the game. I will serve coffee and pumpkin pie.

Philip: *[He leaves.]* OK. I'll be back in a few minutes.

Ellen: Robbie, would you bring the dessert plates. And, Marilyn, would you **pour coffee,¹⁵** please.

Marilyn: Sure, Ellen.

Grandpa: How was your Thanksgiving dinner, Alexandra?

Alexandra: Just wonderful, Mr. Stewart. The Molinas are a large family. I love being with them.

Robbie: I'm glad you came by, Alexandra.

Alexandra: I am, too.

Philip: *[He shouts from the living room.]* Touchdown! Touchdown! Touchdown!

Grandpa: Great Thanksgiving. Lots to be thankful for. Michigan scored a touchdown. Alexandra came by. And nobody misses Philip's famous apple pie.

Ellen: Oh, Grandpa!

END OF ACT III

¹⁴ **How'd . . . ?** = How did . . . ?
¹⁵ **pour coffee:** to serve coffee

ACT III

Activities

Here are some activities to help you check your understanding of this episode.

THANKSGIVING

Use the clues to complete this crossword puzzle.

ACROSS

1. What holiday is it?
7. Alexandra calls Grandpa _____ Stewart.
8. Grandpa said, "The Thanksgiving Day parade is always such great _____."
12. All right
13. There are *touchdowns* in this sport.
15. Ellen said to Philip, ". . . would you join _____ in the kitchen, please?"
16. Cinnamon and pepper are two _____.
17. Philip is Grandpa's _____.
20. Ellen and Philip got _____ early this morning.
22. They celebrated the first Thanksgiving.
24. Robbie said, "Mom! Is it for me?" Ellen said, "_____, Robbie."
25. Grandpa thinks that Robbie was four _____ five years old when they went to the parade together.
26. The Pilgrims arrived in Massachusetts on this ship.
30. Wonderful.
31. Ellen uses Grandma's _____ for turkey dressing.
32. How many people were at the Stewarts' home when it was time for dessert?
33. The oven wasn't _____ because Philip forgot to turn it on.

DOWN

1. A Thanksgiving food
2. Philip enjoys making his "famous Thanksgiving _____ pie."
3. Dressing
4. Ellen keeps the spice rack _____ the kitchen cabinet.
5. Alexandra _____ Robbie's friend.
6. Robbie was grouchy because he missed Alexandra's telephone _____ .
7. Robbie calls his mother _____.
9. The opposite of yes
10. Grandpa said, "Oh, look _____ that float, Robbie."
11. This store organizes a Thanksgiving Day parade.
14. The Michigan football team needed just _____ touchdown to win the game.
18. Grandpa and Robbie watched the parade _____ television.
19. Thanksgiving is in the month of _____.
21. There are _____ in many American cities on Thanksgiving Day.
22. Alexandra brought a _____ pie.
23. I _____ means "I understand."
27. Ellen gave thanks _____ the food on the table.
28. On Thanksgiving, many people _____ college football games.

29. Robbie said, "Alexandra might call. Tell her I'll call her _____ back."
30. Robbie went to the store to _____ some cinnamon.

PREPOSITION DECISIONS

Fill in each blank with a preposition from the box. Use each preposition only once.

1. "Try to come _____ later _____ dessert."
2. "What's gotten _____ him?"
3. ". . . he'll get _____ it."
4. "I look forward _____ seeing you and Harry and Michelle."
5. "What time does the Michigan football game come _____?"

| for |
| by |
| into |
| to |
| on |
| over |

EPISODE 7

"Man's Best Friend"

ACT I

In this episode, you will study . . .

VOCABULARY

cute 聪明的 [kju:t]   ever
shelter 住所或遮蔽   cuddle [kʌdəl] 搂抱
adopt   pet
claim 宣布 要求   pal 伙伴 好朋友

GRAMMAR AND EXPRESSIONS

so and *such*
expressing future possibilities (with *if*)
present perfect verb tense 时态 完成
ordering meat in a restaurant
answering the telephone

ACT II

PRONUNCIATION

the before a vowel sound or a consonant sound

U.S. LIFE

How do Americans feel about their pets?

☞ YOUR TURN

• Do you own a pet?
• What kinds of animals do you like?

ACT III

Here is the complete script with study material for Episode 7. Use these materials before _or_ after you watch.

ACT I

In the Stewarts' home. Robbie Stewart and his friend Alexandra Pappas are listening to music in the living room.

Alexandra: Robbie, this new **Walkman**[1]™ is absolutely wonderful.

Robbie: Richard and Marilyn bought it for me for my birthday.

Alexandra: They're **so**[2] **thoughtful.**[3] You are very lucky, Robbie, to have **such a nice family.**[4]

Robbie: Is something wrong, Alexandra?

Alexandra: No, nothing.

Robbie: Yes, there is. **I can tell.**[5] What's the matter? Come on, you can tell me. **What's up?**[6]

Alexandra: I don't know. Something's wrong.

Robbie: OK, let's talk.

Alexandra: I received a letter from my parents this morning.

Robbie: Did they write some bad news?

Alexandra: No.

Robbie: Well, then why are you so sad?

Alexandra: I miss them. I miss them very much.

Robbie: I'm sorry, Alexandra. But I understand.

Alexandra: The Molinas treat me so nicely, and I love being with your family so much . . . but when I received the letter with photographs of my family, I cried. I cried because I miss them all.

Robbie: You really miss your family, don't you?

Alexandra: Yes. I know I must seem **silly.**[7] It's not like I have nobody. I like the Molinas very much, and they're so kind to me.

Robbie: Hey, why don't we go out for a cheeseburger and french fries? That'll **cheer you up.**[8] And you can use my Walkman.

Alexandra: That's a good idea. But **if we go**[9] out, please don't complain about your math teacher or your math homework. I want to have fun.

Robbie: So do I. *[He begins to turn off the lights.]* I have to turn off the lights, **or else**[10] my father will **get**[11] really angry. He says I never turn them out when I leave. If they come home and they're on . . . *[He moves his index finger across his throat to show that his father will be angry.]*

[1] **Walkman:** a small radio and tape player with earphones

Walkman™ *personal stereo* is a registered trademark of the Sony Corporation.

[2] **so:** very
So is more emotional than *very*.

[3] **thoughtful:** kind

[4] **such a nice family:** a very nice family.
Such a is more emotional than *a very*. Use *such a* before an adjective and a singular noun.

[5] **I can tell.** = I can see.

[6] **What's up?** = What's happening?
This is a very popular expression.

[7] **silly:** ridiculous

[8] **cheer you up:** to make you feel happier

[9] **if we go**
To refer to a future possibility after *if*, use a present verb form (*go*, not *will go*).

[10] **or else:** if not
Here, this phrase means "if I don't turn off the lights."

[11] **get:** to become
Get often has this meaning before an adjective or an adverb describing an adjective.

[*There is a sound at the patio door.*]

Robbie: Do you hear something?

Alexandra: Yes. What was that?

Robbie: It sounded like a dog **barking.**[12]

Alexandra: It sounded like a dog barking right here.

Robbie: Yeah. [*He opens the door. A dog is standing there.*]

Alexandra: A dog!

Robbie: A **springer spaniel!**[13] [*to the dog*] Come on in! Make yourself at home.

Alexandra: Oh, you poor little thing. Come here.

Robbie: Come on.

Alexandra: Poor baby.

Robbie: Where did *you* come from?

Alexandra: [*She looks at the dog's identification tag.*] Her name's Gemma, and she belongs to Mr. and Mrs. Levinson. There's a phone number—five five five . . . eight four four eight. Robbie, maybe you should call them and tell the Levinsons we have their **cute**[14] little spaniel.

Robbie: **I've always wanted**[15] a springer spaniel. She's so cute. [*He goes to the telephone and dials the Levinsons' number.*]

Operator: The number you are calling—555-8448— is **no longer in service.**[16]

Robbie: [*He hangs up the phone.*] The number's no longer in service.

Alexandra: [*to the dog*] Oh, you poor, poor baby. **You've lost**[17] your family.

Robbie: We'll find them. Don't worry, Alexandra.

END OF ACT I

12 **barking:** the loud sounds that a dog makes

13 **springer spaniel:** a type of dog

14 **cute:** pretty or attractive, like a child

15 **I've always wanted . . . =** I have always wanted . . .
Have wanted is in the present perfect verb tense. This tense (*have/has* + past participle) refers to a time *before now* or *until now,* with a focus on the present. In other words, the present perfect always connects the past to the present.

16 **no longer in service:** not working anymore

17 **You've lost . . . =** You have lost . . .
Here, Alexandra uses the present perfect verb tense because *losing* the family is *before now,* but Alexandra is thinking of the dog's *present* lonely condition.

ACT I

Activities

Here are some activities to help you check your understanding of Act I.

"SO" AND "SUCH"

We use *so* or *such* instead of *very* to add more emotion.
Use *so* before an adjective or an adverb.

Use *such* before an adjective and a plural noun.
Use *such a* before an adjective and a singular noun.

EXAMPLES: The dog is **so** cute.
The Molinas treat Alexandra **so nicely**.
EXAMPLE: Springer spaniels are **such** cute dogs.
EXAMPLE: Gemma is **such a** cute dog.

Complete Robbie's sentences correctly. Write *so, such,* or *such a* in each blank.

1. Alexandra and I are _____ good friends.
2. Alexandra was _____ unhappy, and I didn't understand why at first.
3. I asked her, "Why are you _____ sad?"
4. We always have _____ good time when we go out together.
5. Gemma looked _____ lonely . . . with _____ sad face.

A DIFFERENT "SO"

We can also use the word *so* in a completely different way—to mean "for that reason" or "therefore."
EXAMPLE: Alexandra received a letter from her family, **so** she began to miss her family more.

Draw a line from the beginning part of each sentence to the correct ending at the right. The first answer is given.

1. Robbie got a new Walkman, *so*
2. Alexandra missed her family, *so*
3. The Molinas are kind to Alexandra, *so*
4. Robbie wanted to cheer up Alexandra, *so*
5. Alexandra just wanted to have fun, *so*
6. They heard something at the door, *so*
7. There was a phone number on the dog tag, *so*

a. she likes them very much.
b. she asked Robbie not to complain about math.
c. he wanted Alexandra to hear it.
d. Robbie went to open it.
e. Robbie dialed the number.
f. he suggested going out for some food.
g. she cried.

ACT II

A little later. Robbie and Alexandra are in the kitchen. They are feeding the dog.

Robbie: Don't worry, Alexandra. We'll find **the owner**.¹

Alexandra: How, Robbie?

Robbie: Let me think.

Alexandra: *[to the dog]* Gemma, sit. Good Gemma. Give me your **paw**.² Good Gemma. This dog is **well trained**.³

Robbie: She likes you, too.

Alexandra: So how are we going to find the owners?

Robbie: With a little help from the ASPCA, the American Society for the Prevention of Cruelty to Animals. They're the ones. We once found a cat. She was caught in the **branches**⁴ of our tree. And Dad called the ASPCA. They came and solved the problem.

Alexandra: Robbie, let's call them.

[Robbie looks up the number in the telephone book.]

Robbie: Let me see—ASPCA. . . . Here it is. ASPCA Animal **Shelter**.⁵ 555-7700. *[He calls.]*

Linda: Hello, ASPCA.

Robbie: Hello, my name is Robbie Stewart. I have a lost dog I'd like to bring to you. **How late are you open?**⁶

Linda: We're open till nine P.M.

¹ **the owner**
Before a vowel sound (like ō in *owner*), pronounce *the* as *thee* [thē].

² **paw:** the foot of an animal with four feet

³ **well trained:** taught to follow directions correctly

⁴ **branches:**

⁵ **shelter:** a temporary home or place for protection

⁶ **How late are you open?** = Until what time are you open?

Robbie:	Thank you. I'll bring the dog **over**[7] by nine.
Linda:	Thanks. Bye.
Robbie:	Thanks. Good-bye. *[He hangs up the phone.]*
Alexandra:	They're still open?
Robbie:	They're open until nine o'clock. We have two and a half hours. Let's take Gemma **by**[8] there now. They'll find the owner.
Alexandra:	I hope so. I'm so sad to see this little dog without her family.
Robbie:	I'm sure they'll find the owner. But if they don't, I'll **adopt**[9] her. She's so cute. Look at those eyes. She's **hard to resist.**[10] Don't you just love her?
Alexandra:	I'd like to keep her, too. But I'll be going home to Greece at the end of the semester. She just wants love and **affection.**[11] Come on, Robbie. Let's get her to the animal shelter, so they can find her owners quickly. *[to the dog]* Don't worry, Gemma. We'll **get**[12] you home. It's not easy being away from home.
Robbie:	Come on, **poochie.**[13] **Atta girl!**[14] Let's go. **We're off**[15] to the animal shelter.

At the ASPCA Animal Shelter. Robbie and Alexandra are in the office of the shelter's director, Linda Aborn.

Linda:	*[She writes on a form.]* Your name?
Robbie:	Robbie Stewart. And this is Alexandra Pappas.
Linda:	*Your* name **will do,**[16] Mr. Stewart. Your address?
Robbie:	46 Linden Street, Riverdale.
Linda:	Where did you find the dog?
Alexandra:	She found us.
Linda:	You tried calling the number on the **collar?**[17]
Robbie:	Yes, but the number's no longer in service.
Linda:	And there's no address on the dog tag?
Alexandra:	There's no other information.
Linda:	No **ID**[18] number. Without that, it's hard.
Alexandra:	You *will* try to find the dog's owner.
Linda:	Oh, we'll try, believe me.
Robbie:	And if you don't?
Linda:	Yes?
Robbie:	If you don't . . . can I . . . can I adopt the dog?

[7] **over;** [8] **by:** to that place

[9] **adopt:** to take into one's family

[10] **hard to resist:** very attractive; difficult not to like

[11] **affection:** a gentle, caring feeling

[12] **get:** to take

[13] **poochie:** dog
This is an informal word. *Pooch* is more usual than *poochie.*

[14] **Atta girl!** = That's a good girl!
Atta girl! and *Atta boy!* are very informal expressions. You use these expressions with animals or children to show that they are doing something well.

[15] **We're off.** = We're going; we're on our way.

[16] **will do:** will be enough

[17] **collar:** a leather band for a dog's neck

[18] **ID:** identification
ID is the abbreviation, or short form, for *identification.*

Linda: Why, yes. If the owners don't **claim**[19] the dog in forty-eight hours, then you can apply for adoption.

Robbie: How **do**[20] I do that?

Alexandra: You really want to?

Robbie: Yes, I'm serious. If no one comes to claim Gemma, I'd like to adopt her.

Linda: It's not difficult.

END OF ACT II

---

[19] **claim:** to say that one owns something

[20] **do:** can or should

You can use *do* in this way to ask for instructions.

U.S. LIFE

The ASPCA (American Society for the Prevention of Cruelty to Animals) began in New York in 1866. This group works to protect animals. In the United States, there are laws against treating animals badly. The ASPCA investigates cases against people who are cruel to animals to be sure that these people are punished. The ASPCA has its own animal shelters and animal hospitals. It also inspects places where many animals are kept to be sure that these animals are cared for. The United States has about 600 societies like the ASPCA.

☞ YOUR TURN

- Are there groups similar to the ASPCA in your country?
- Do you think a government should make laws to protect the rights of animals? Why, or why not?
- Do you agree that people who are cruel to animals should be punished?

ACT II ▶ *Activities*

Here are some activities to help you check your understanding of Act II.

PRONUNCIATION

There are two pronunciations of the word *the*. You hear "the" [thə] before a consonant sound and "thee" [thē] (with a long ē sound) before a vowel sound. Remember that the pronunciation of *the* depends on the *sound* that follows it.

Read the following sentences. Connect the word *the* to the following vowel sound every time it needs a long ē sound. Use a curved line( ). The first answer is given.

1. The director at the ᴗASPCA is very helpful.
2. The problem is they need to find the owner of the dog.
3. The hour is very late, but the animal shelter is open till nine.
4. Robbie has the idea to adopt Gemma if the owners (the Levinsons) don't call the office.

CROSSWORD

Fill in this crossword puzzle.

ACROSS
2. Robbie lives in _____, New York.
4. Gemma is a _____.
7. Robbie would like to _____ Gemma.
9. The Levinsons are Gemma's _____.
12. _____ is Robbie's friend.
13. Gemma misses her _____, and Alexandra misses hers, too.

DOWN
1. Alexandra is from _____.
3. _____ has a new Walkman.
5. Linda Aborn's office is _____ until nine o'clock.
6. Gemma has an ID tag on her _____.
7. The _____ helps animals.
8. Linda Aborn will try to _____ the Levinsons.
10. Robbie remembered when a _____ was caught in the branches of a tree.
11. If no one comes to _____ Gemma in forty-eight hours, Robbie might keep her.

ACT III

At the animal shelter later that day. Robbie and Alexandra are still talking with Linda Aborn.

Linda: OK. If you want to adopt an animal, first we need to know some **references.**[1]

Robbie: References? People we know?

Linda: Friends, teachers. . . . We need to talk to some people about you. We want to be sure that you're responsible and that you can take good care of an animal. Then you have to **fill out**[2] this form about your **family background.**[3]

Robbie: **Is that it?**[4]

Linda: No, there's more. We need to know about your history with animals. Have you **ever**[5] owned an animal?

Robbie: Yes. We had a cat when I was eight years old. I love cats.

Linda: Do you have any animals now?

Robbie: **Unfortunately,**[6] no.

Alexandra: Anything else?

Linda: We also like to know your reasons for wanting an animal.

Alexandra: Just to hold it and **cuddle**[7] with it. Just to have as a **pet.**[8] I love animals.

Robbie: To have a friend—a **pal.**[9] You know, **man's best friend**[10] is his dog.

Linda: And one thing more. If you're under twenty-one years of age . . .

Robbie: That's me.

Linda: Then an **adult**[11] must sign for you.

Alexandra: Uh-oh.

Robbie: No problem. My parents will think it's a good idea. I'll **be back**[12] with them.

Alexandra: If the real owners don't come to claim Gemma . . .

Linda: After forty-eight hours. But please call first.

Robbie: Thanks for your information and for being so helpful.

Linda: It's my pleasure. Nice talking to both of you.

[1] **references:** people or statements that can give information about someone

[2] **fill out:** to complete

[3] **family background:** family history and information

[4] **Is that it?** = Is that all?

[5] **ever:** at any time

[6] **unfortunately:** I'm sorry to say

[7] **cuddle:** to hold in a gentle, loving way

[8] **pet:** an animal that one usually keeps at home

[9] **pal:** a close friend

[10] **man's best friend**
This phrase means that a dog can be a person's closest companion.

[11] **adult:** a person twenty-one years of age or older

[12] **be back:** to return

[They start to leave.]

Robbie: Thanks again. Bye.

Alexandra: Maybe the real owners will come to claim her.

Robbie: Her eyes look so sad. She must really miss them.

Linda: I see you're both animal lovers.

Robbie: We are.

Alexandra: Good-bye, Miss Aborn. We'll call in a couple of days.

Linda: Good-bye, and thanks for bringing Gemma in.

Robbie: Bye.

Inside Perriello's Restaurant later that day. Robbie and Alexandra are sitting in a booth. They are going to order dinner.

Alexandra: I keep thinking about the dog—about Gemma, alone in the animal shelter.

Robbie: I know. But I promise you, Alexandra, the dog is just fine. They're very kind to the animals.

Alexandra: I know they are. I mean about her being alone. Even if they are kind to Gemma, she's still alone, without her family.

[The waiter comes to take their order.]

Waiter: Ready, **folks?**[13]

Robbie: Are you ready, Alexandra?

Alexandra: Yes, I'm ready. I'll have the **chef's salad,**[14] please.

Robbie: I will have a cheeseburger, **medium rare,**[15] with **raw**[16] onion, and french fries, please.

Waiter: Anything to drink?

Alexandra: A diet cola, please.

Robbie: Ginger ale with lots of ice for me, thank you.

Waiter: I've got it. Thanks.

Robbie: Aren't you surprised that the animal shelter is so careful about finding homes for the animals?

Alexandra: No, I'm not.

[The waiter returns with their food.]

Waiter: And a cheeseburger, medium rare, with onion and french fries. And a ginger ale with lots of ice. Salad dressing?

[13] **folks:** people
This is a friendly, informal word.

[14] **chef's salad:** a large salad, usually with lettuce, tomato, turkey, ham, and cheese

[15] **medium rare:** a way to order a hamburger or a steak

well done	cooked very much
medium well	
medium	
medium rare	
rare	not completely cooked

[16] **raw:** not cooked

A little later at the restaurant. Robbie and Alexandra are eating.

Robbie: Hey, I wanted you to hear my new sound system when the dog scratched on the front door. Let's finish eating, and then we'll go back to my house. I want you to hear my new tapes. I've got some great new dance music.

In the Stewarts' home later that night. Robbie and Alexandra are dancing. The phone rings. Robbie answers it.

Robbie: Hello. **Stewart residence.**[17]
Linda: Hello. Is Robbie Stewart there?
Robbie: **This is he.**[18] Who's this?
Linda: This is Linda Aborn from the animal shelter.
Robbie: *[to Alexandra]* It's Linda from the animal shelter. Yes, Linda. Hi.
Linda: We have good news and bad news, Robbie.
Robbie: Oh?
Linda: The good news is that the Levinsons have come by to pick up the dog. The bad news is, you won't be able to adopt the dog.
Robbie: That's OK.
Linda: Come by one day and look at some of the other dogs. I'm sure there's one for you. Thanks, Robbie. And the Levinsons thank you for bringing their dog to us.
Robbie: Thanks, Linda. Bye. *[He hangs up.]*
Alexandra: The owners claimed Gemma?
Robbie: That's right.
Alexandra: I'm glad for the dog.
Robbie: I guess I am, too. She said if I come by, she'll help me find another dog.
Alexandra: *[She smiles.]* Come on. Let's dance.

END OF ACT III

[17] **Stewart residence:** the home of the Stewarts
This is a formal way to answer the telephone.

[18] **This is he.** = This is Robbie Stewart.
This is he or *This is she* is a frequent response when a caller asks to speak to the person who answers the telephone.

U.S. LIFE

Dogs, cats, birds, and fish are common pets in American homes. Americans often think of a pet as one of the family. Many people believe that taking care of a pet helps children learn responsibility. For this reason, many classrooms have small pets, such as rabbits or frogs.

rabbit   **frog**

☞ YOUR TURN

• Which pets are common in your country?
• Do you have a pet? If not, would you like to own one?
• What kinds of animals do you like? Are there any animals that you don't like?

ACT III **Activities**

Here are some activities to help you check your understanding of this episode.

PETS IN THE U.S.A.

How many of these pets can you name? Try to find the correct name in the box. Then write the name of the pet on the line below each picture.

bird
cat
rabbit
fish
dog

1. _____

2. _____

3. _____

4. _____

5. _____

DIFFERENT REFERENCES

What is the reference for the <u>underlined</u> pronoun in each of the following lines from this episode? Circle *a* or *b*.

1. In Act I, Robbie says, "Richard and Marilyn bought <u>it</u> for me for my birthday."
   a. the Walkman   **b.** the dog

2. In Act I, Robbie says, "Did <u>they</u> write some bad news?"
   a. Robbie's parents   **b.** Alexandra's parents

3. In Act II, Robbie says, "<u>We</u> once found a cat."
   a. Robbie and Alexandra   **b.** the Stewart family

4. In Act II, Robbie says, "I'm sure <u>they</u>'ll find the owner."
   a. the ASPCA   **b.** the Levinsons

5. In Act II, Alexandra says, "<u>She</u> found us."
   a. Linda Aborn   **b.** Gemma

6. In Act III, Linda says, "And the Levinsons thank you for bringing their dog to <u>us</u>."
   a. Robbie and Alexandra   **b.** the ASPCA

EPISODE 8

"You're Going to Be Fine"

ACT I

In this episode you will study . . .

VOCABULARY

scheduling
infected
reassurance

cold
sore throat
charades

GRAMMAR AND EXPRESSIONS

present tense with future meaning
talking about health
tag questions

PRONUNCIATION

basic vowel sounds

ACT II

 U.S. LIFE

How do Americans pay for medical care?

☞ YOUR TURN

• Who pays for medical care in your country?
• How often do you see a doctor?

ACT III

Here is the complete script with study material for Episode 8. Use these materials before *or* after you watch.

ACT I

Outside Lawrence Hospital one morning. Inside, Dr. Philip Stewart and his nurse, Molly Baker, are working in Dr. Stewart's office.

Philip: Molly, I need your special talent for **handling**[1] special matters.

Molly: Like what special matters?

Philip: Well, I have a **scheduling**[2] problem.

Molly: Yes?

Philip: I have three **tonsillectomies**[3] set for Friday with Dr. Earl.

Molly: Yes?

Philip: I need to fit a fourth operation into his schedule. And . . . I know you can do it.

Molly: Who's the patient?

Philip: Carl Herrera. The boy has **infected**[4] tonsils, and we should **remove**[5] them as soon as possible.

Molly: Well, I'll try to arrange the schedule, Dr. Stewart. But it's not going to be easy.

Philip: I know you'll be able to take care of it.

[Molly shakes her head and laughs.]

Inside Dr. Stewart's office later that day. Philip is talking to a mother, Mrs. Herrera, and her ten-year-old son Carl.

Philip: *[He looks at Carl's medical chart.]* Well, Mrs. Herrera, Carl will be perfectly fine after we remove his tonsils.

Mother: Thank you for your **reassurance**,[6] Dr. Stewart. He's had so many **colds**[7] and **sore throats**[8] recently.

Philip: Well, it's a very easy operation, Carl. You won't feel a thing.

Carl: But when **do**[9] they do it?

Philip: This Friday.

Carl: But Saturday's my birthday.

Philip: *[He looks at his appointment book.]* Well, we could **reschedule**[10] the operation, Mrs. Herrera, but I don't want to **put it off**[11] too long.

[1] **handling:** taking care of

[2] **scheduling:** planning for things to happen at a certain time

[3] **tonsillectomies:** operations to take out the *tonsils*

tonsils

[4] **infected:** diseased

[5] **remove:** to take out

[6] **reassurance:** words to make someone feel less afraid

[7] **colds:** sicknesses with coughing and sneezing

coughing   sneezing

[8] **sore throats**
This boy has a *sore throat*. His throat hurts.

[9] **do:** will
You sometimes use the simple present tense to refer to future schedules.

[10] **reschedule:** to schedule again; change the time for an appointment

[11] **put (it) off:** to delay (the operation) until a later time; postpone (it)

Mother:	No, I think it's important to do it now. We can have a birthday party for you, Carl, **when you come**[12] out of the hospital.
Carl:	But it won't be on my birthday.
Mother:	But your health is more important, Carl, believe me.
Carl:	I don't want my tonsils out.
Philip:	*[He buzzes Molly on the intercom.]* Nurse Baker, would you come in, please?
Molly:	*[She enters.]* Hello, Mrs. Herrera. Hi, Carl, **how you doing?**[13]
Carl:	I don't want my tonsils out.
Molly:	Come with me, Carl. You and I will **talk this over.**[14] *[She leaves the room with Carl.]*
Mother:	She has a special way with kids.
Philip:	She sure does.

In an area of the hospital. Carl is sitting on a sofa. He is unhappy. Molly enters and tries to make him feel better. She is carrying a robe and pajamas for him.

Molly:	Carl, does your throat hurt?
Carl:	Yes.
Molly:	OK. Do you want to get better?
Carl:	Yes.
Molly:	OK. We want you to get better, too. You'll have your tonsils out tomorrow, and you won't get so many colds anymore.
Carl:	But if I have my tonsils out tomorrow, I'll miss my birthday party on Saturday.
Molly:	I know. **It's a problem, isn't it?**[15] Let me try to **work something out.**[16]
Carl:	What?
Molly:	I have to think about it.
Carl:	You're **fooling**[17] me.
Molly:	Oh, I'm not, Carl. Give me a chance to think about it, and I'll **come up with**[18] something.
Carl:	A surprise?
Molly:	Maybe. But you just put on your pajamas and robe, and I'll think of a surprise.
Carl:	Will it hurt?
Molly:	No. There are other boys and girls here, and they're having their tonsils out. You'll meet them.
Carl:	I don't want to.
Molly:	Change your clothes, Carl. Everything will be just fine.

END OF ACT I

12 when you come
After *when,* use a present verb form (*come,* not *will come*) to refer to future time. Also, use a present-tense verb with future meaning to follow these words and phrases: *after, before, if, unless, until, while, as soon as,* and *in case.*

13 How you doing? = How are you doing? *or* How're you doing?
This is a very informal way to ask, "How are you?"

14 talk (this) over: to discuss (something)

15 It's a problem, isn't it? = It's a problem, right?
This is an example of a *tag question.* Use tag questions to check information.

16 work (something) out: to find an answer to a problem

17 fooling: joking with; kidding

18 come up with: to get a new idea; invent

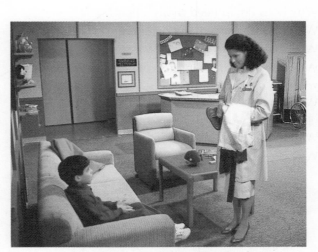

" . . . just put on your pajamas and robe . . . "

ACT I

Activities

Here are some activities to help you check your understanding of Act I.

TALKING ABOUT HEALTH

What is bothering the person in each picture? What is he saying? Choose the correct answer from the box. Then write the answer in the speech balloon above the correct picture. The first answer is given.

| I have a headache. | I have a stomachache. | I have a sore throat. | I have a fever. | I have a cold. |

WHY? BECAUSE . . .

Draw a line from each sentence at the left to the correct answer at the right. The first answer is given.

1. Why does Philip need Molly's help?
2. Why does Carl need an operation?
3. Why does Mrs. Herrera feel reassured?
4. Why doesn't Carl want to have the operation this week?
5. Why doesn't Mrs. Herrera want to put off the operation?
6. Why does Mrs. Herrera like the nurse?
7. Why doesn't Molly tell Carl more about the surprise?

a. Because his birthday is on Saturday.
b. Because Philip tells her that Carl will be fine.
c. Because she thinks it's important to do it now.
d. Because he has a scheduling problem.
e. Because she has to think about it first.
f. Because he has infected tonsils.
g. Because Molly is good with children.

ACT II

In the hospital the next day. Now there are four children, including Carl. Molly enters and tries to amuse them.

Molly: OK. Do you know how to play **charades?**[1]

[Betty and Tim raise their hands.]

Molly: Frank, you've never played charades?

Frank: Nope.

Molly: Carl, you're sure you've never played?

[Carl shakes his head no.]

Molly: OK, Betty, Tim, and Frank. We're going to play charades. Frank, you can learn as we go. And, Carl, you **join in**[2] at any time. OK, let me think. OK, I've got one. *[She writes a title on a piece of paper. She puts the paper on a table so that no one can see the title.]* All right. *[She makes the charades motion for "movie" by pretending to hold an old-fashioned camera in her left hand and turning the handle with her right hand.]*

Betty: A movie! A movie!

Molly: *[She touches her nose with her index finger. This means "correct" in charades.]* Right. A movie. OK. *[She counts to six on her fingers because there are are six words in the title of the movie. Then she holds up six fingers.]*

Tim: Six words. It has six words.

Frank: That's easy. I can play.

Molly: Good. OK. We've got a movie. The title . . .

Betty: Six words.

Molly: Right. First word . . . *[She pulls her ear. This means "sounds like" in charades.]*

Betty: Sounds like.

Tim: Sounds like . . .

Molly: You got that part right. Yes. *[pulling her ear]* Sounds like . . . *[She shakes her head no.]* Sounds like what?

Frank: Sounds like *no.*

Molly: *[touching her nose]* Absolutely right, Frank. Sounds like *no.* OK. We've got a movie. Six words. The first word sounds like *no.*

Tim, Betty, Frank, and Carl

[1] **charades:** a guessing game
In *charades,* one person silently acts out a name, a title, or a phrase while other players try to guess it. For example, to show the word *understand,* a player might act out *under* and *stand.*

[2] **join in:** to do it with us

"OK, I've got one."

"A movie."

"Sounds like . . ."

Frank: Row. Row.

Tim: Go.

Molly: Nope.

Tim: Show. That's it—show.

Molly: *[laughing]* No . . . OK . . . *[She acts out the word* snow *with her fingers.]*

Betty: *[quickly]* Snow.

Molly: *[She touches her nose.]* Absolutely right, Betty. Sounds like *no—snow.* OK, a movie. Six words. The first word is *snow.*

Frank: This is fun.

[Carl doesn't think so.]

Molly: Oh, OK. *[She holds up five fingers.]*

Betty: The fifth word.

Molly: Right, fifth word. *[She holds up seven fingers.]*

Tim: Seven?

Molly: *[She touches her nose.]* Absolutely right. Very good. The fifth word is *seven.* OK, we've got a movie. The first word is *snow.* Fifth word, *seven.*

Betty: **I got it!**[3] I got it!

Frank: ***Snow White and the Seven Dwarfs.***[4]

[Molly shows the piece of paper with the title.]

Betty: I got it.

Frank: *I* got it.

Molly: Frank, you got it. Betty, you had it, but you didn't say it.

Tim: I knew it.

Molly: Carl, now you know charades. Why don't you join us?

Carl: I don't like charades. It's for babies.

Molly: Oh, I like it.

Carl: Well, they're babies.

Betty: You're a **sore loser.**[5]

Tim: Yeah.

[3] **I got it!** = I have the answer. This is an informal expression.

[4] ***Snow White and the Seven Dwarfs:*** the title of a popular children's story, or fairy tale, and movie

[5] **sore loser:** someone who acts badly after losing a game

Molly: No **arguing.**[6] Save your voices. Between now and tomorrow you're all going to have your tonsils out. And you won't be able to speak for a while. So save your voices till then. *[She points to her throat.]*

Philip: *[He enters.]* Hi, **gang.**[7] Hi, everybody. Well, what's **going on?**[8]

Molly: I sure am glad to see you, Dr. Stewart. *[joking]* This is a rough group.

Carl: I didn't want to play charades, so they're angry at me.

Philip: Why don't you want to play?

Carl: Because I don't want to be here. I don't want my tonsils out.

Philip: Why not?

Carl: Because my birthday is tomorrow. My mother **promised me**[9] a birthday party with a clown.

Molly: But you can have one when you go home, Carl.

Carl: But my birthday is tomorrow.

Philip: I'm sorry, Carl.

Molly: Carl, you'll have your party when you go home.

Carl: But it won't be on my birthday! *[to Molly]* And you promised me a surprise.

END OF ACT II

[6] **arguing:** strongly disagreeing

[7] **gang:** a group of people
This is an informal word.

[8] **going on:** happening

[9] **promised me:** agreed to give me

ACT II

Activities

Here are some activities to help you check your understanding of Act II.

PRONUNCIATION

There are eleven basic vowel sounds in American English. In the box, there are two examples of words with each of these sounds. Read each group of three words below. Circle the one word with a vowel sound that is different from the vowel sound in the other two words. If you wish, you may use a dictionary for this activity.

EXAMPLE: low   so   (raw)

(*Low* and *so* have the same vowel sound [ō]; *law* has a different vowel sound [ô].)

[ē]	feet	seat
[i]	fit	sit
[ā]	late	pain
[e]	let	pen
[a]	hat	sack
[u]	luck	shut
[o]	lock	shot
[o͞o]	food	pool
[oo]	foot	pull
[ō]	so	boat
[ô]	saw	bought

1. bowl   whole   ball
2. hot   rock   hat
3. seat   sick   need
4. good   book   soon
5. head   men   made
6. song   note   hope
7. run   pull   but
8. done   love   gone

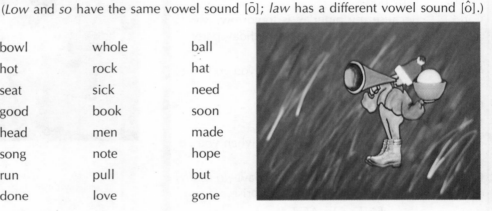

CHARADES

Let's play *charades*. Look at the five pictures. In pictures 1, 2, 4, and 5, the person is acting out a clue for a word. An extra clue is given below each picture. Try to guess each word. Then add the words together to get the name of a "famous doctor." Write this name in the box at the bottom of the page. The third sound (*s*) is given.

S

1. He wants to _____ the glass.
2. He's touching his _____.
3.
4. He's holding up _____ fingers.
5. He's feeling his _____.

ACT III

Outside Lawrence Hospital. Then, inside the hospital on Friday afternoon. The four children have had their tonsils out. They are sad, and their throats hurt. Molly enters, and she talks to Betty first.

Molly: It hurts, doesn't it?

[Betty nods her head yes.]

Molly: You'll feel better tomorrow, Betty, believe me. Only one day, and it won't hurt as much. Do you feel like eating? Having some dinner? Oh, don't look so sad. Let me tell you about your dinner. It's ice cream.

[Betty smiles.]

Molly: Ice cream. All kinds of flavors. Chocolate.

[Betty shakes her head no.]

Molly: Strawberry?

[Betty nods yes.]

Molly: Vanilla?

[Betty nods yes again.]

Molly: Vanilla, too?

[Betty smiles.]

Molly: I see you're feeling better already, Betty. So you *will* have dinner?

[Betty agrees she will.]

Molly: OK, honey, we'll **see to it**[1] that you have strawberry and vanilla ice cream. Just rest now. You need some rest to help you get better quickly. *[She walks over to Frank.]* Hi, Frank. How you doing?

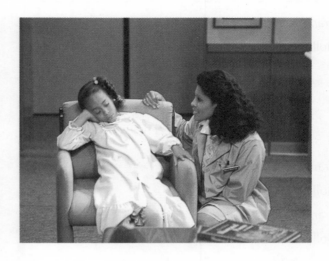

[1] **see to it:** to be sure (to do something)

[Frank is not doing very well.]

Molly: Oh, **come on**[2] now. You're a big boy. It doesn't hurt that much, does it? *[She sees that he is in pain.]* Oh, I'm sorry it hurts so much, and you won't be able to have dinner. You're just going to have to have ice cream. Yes, ice cream. Lots of flavors. **Want to hear them?**[3]

[Frank nods his head yes.]

Molly: Chocolate?

[Frank loves chocolate, and he smiles.]

Molly: Then chocolate it is. One scoop or two?

[Frank holds up three fingers.]

Molly: *Three* scoops?

[Frank nods.]

Molly: Then three it will be.

[She walks over to Tim, and he holds up three fingers.]

Molly: You want three scoops also?

[He nods.]

Molly: Chocolate, too?

[He nods.]

Molly: Well, I see you're feeling better.

[He shakes his head no.]

Molly: Well, at least you're acting like you feel better. Three scoops of chocolate ice cream for Tim **coming up**[4] *[She now moves over to Carl. He also is not feeling well.]* Hi, Carl. How you doing?

[Carl points to his throat.]

Molly: I know it hurts. But it'll be better tomorrow. In the meantime, what would you like?

Carl: Surprise.

Molly: A surprise? I promised you a surprise, didn't I? And it wasn't just ice cream, was it?

[2] **come on:** stop acting like that

[3] **Want to hear them?** = Do you want to hear the flavors?

[4] **coming up:** coming very soon
You might use this informal phrase when you are going to serve food or a drink.

[*Carl can't say another word. It is difficult for him to speak.*]

Molly: Your birthday is tomorrow, isn't it?

[*He nods.*]

Molly: Well, maybe, just maybe, there *will* be a surprise. But first you have to smile. I just want to see one smile from you.

[*Carl doesn't smile.*]

Molly: No smile, no surprise. That's the **deal.**[5] No smile, no surprise. If you want a surprise, then you've got to smile first.

[*Carl finally smiles.*]

In the hospital the next day. It's Saturday, Carl's birthday. The children are feeling better. Carl is waiting for his surprise. Molly enters.

Molly: How you all doing? Well, I'm glad you're feeling better because we have a little surprise for you today. It's Carl's birthday [*Carl smiles*], and we have Popo the Clown to entertain you. And here he is—Popo the Clown.

[*Molly waves her hand, and a clown comes into the room. The children watch the clown, and they become happy. A little later, Philip and Mrs. Herrera enter. They are wheeling a table with bowls of ice cream on it.*]

Philip: Happy birthday, Carl. Happy birthday. All right, everybody. OK, Carl. It's your birthday. What's your wish? What would you like?

[*Carl pulls his ear. Then he points to his nose.*]

Philip: Hmm? [*He doesn't understand.*]

Molly: [*She understands.*] You want to play charades?

[*They all laugh and clap their hands.*]

END OF ACT III

5 **deal:** an agreement

U.S. LIFE

In the United States, about 7 million people work in the medical-care system, the largest field of employment in the country. There are 450,000 doctors, 1 million registered nurses, 120,000 dentists, and 150,000 pharmacists. Most doctors in the United States are in private practice. This means that their medical office is organized like a business.

Most Americans have private health insurance to pay their medical bills. But this insurance covers less than 40% of medical costs. The people must pay for the rest of the costs. A government program called **Medicare** helps to pay medical bills for people over age sixty-five.

☞ YOUR TURN

- Who pays for medical care in your country?
- Do most doctors in your country work for the government?
- How often do you see a doctor? About how much does a visit to a doctor cost?

ACT III

Activities

Here are some activities to help you check your understanding of this episode.

TAG QUESTIONS

To check information, you can use a *tag question:* an auxiliary and a pronoun at the end of a sentence. You use a tag question when you think that you already know the answer. A tag question means "Right?" Study the examples and explanations below. Then complete exercises *A* and *B*.

Molly *is* a good nurse, *isn't she?*
Carl *isn't* sad now, *is he?*
Carl *will* always remember this birthday, *won't he?*
He *won't* forget Popo the Clown, *will he?*
Betty *was* sick, *wasn't she?*
Tim *wasn't* feeling too bad, *was he?*

→ If the verb or auxiliary in the sentence is positive *(is, will, was)*, use a negative auxiliary *(isn't, won't, wasn't)* and the correct subject pronoun; if the verb or auxiliary in the sentence is negative *(isn't, won't, wasn't)*, use a positive auxiliary *(is, will, was)* and the correct subject pronoun.

Negative sentences with *don't, doesn't,* and *didn't* follow the rule above for tag questions.

The children *don't* have a fever now, *do they?*
Frank's throat *doesn't* hurt too much, *does it?*
Philip *didn't* have ice cream, *did he?*

But positive sentences with simple, *-s,* and past verb forms have no auxiliaries. For these sentences, follow the rules for tag questions below.

The children *like* ice cream, *don't they?*
You *eat* ice cream, *don't you?*

→ If the main verb is in the simple form *(like, eat),* use *don't* in the tag question.

Molly *wants* the children to feel better, *doesn't she?*
Carl *likes* to play charades, *doesn't he?*

→ If the main verb is in the *-s* form *(wants, likes),* use *doesn't* in the tag question.

Betty *asked* for two ice-cream flavors, *didn't she?*
The children *had* fun, *didn't they?*

→ If the main verb is in the past form *(asked, had),* use *didn't* in the tag question.

A. Read the script for Act III to find the five sentences with tag questions. Write those five sentences on the blank lines.

1. _____   4. _____

2. _____   5. _____

3. _____

B. Add the correct tag question to each of the following sentences. For each sentence, use one of the tag questions in the boxes above. Be sure to use the correct subject pronoun.

1. Carl's birthday is on Saturday, _____?
2. He wasn't happy about being in the hospital,_____?
3. Philip will thank Molly for her help, _____?
4. She helps Philip a lot, _____?
5. The children learned how to play charades, _____?
6. The children like the game, _____?
7. They didn't expect to see a clown, _____?
8. Popo was funny, _____?

"It's Up to You"

ACT I

In this episode, you will study . . .

VOCABULARY

applicant
transcript
journalist
tuition

GRAMMAR AND EXPRESSIONS

comparative and superlative adjectives

PRONUNCIATION

intonation of information questions
stress of prepositions in sentences

ACT II

U.S. LIFE

- What is the difference between a college and a university?
- What are the entrance requirements for American colleges or universities?
- What are some liberal arts subjects?

☞ YOUR TURN

- How do students apply to colleges or universities in your country?
- Do students in your country usually leave home when they go to college?

ACT III

Here is the complete script with study material for Episode 9. Use these materials before *or* after you watch.

ACT I

In Robbie Stewart's room one evening. Robbie is working at his computer. He hears a knock at the door.

Robbie: Who is it?

Philip: Dad.

Robbie: Come on in, Dad.

Philip: I thought you might be hungry. I brought you a chicken sandwich and a glass of milk.

Robbie: I *am* hungry. Thanks, Dad. What time is it, **anyway?¹**

Philip: *[He looks at his watch.]* Ten o'clock. **What are you working on?²**

Robbie: I'm writing a story for the high-school **paper.³**

Philip: Can't you finish it tomorrow?

Robbie: No, I have to **turn it in⁴** in the morning.

Philip: **What's it about?⁵**

Robbie: I'm writing an **article⁶** on the feelings about graduation.

Philip: And . . . how do you feel?

Robbie: Me? A little **scared.⁷** And excited, too.

Philip: I felt the same way.

Robbie: The **scary⁸** part's leaving home and moving to college.

Philip: Oh, leaving home is part of growing up. Well, don't work all night.

Robbie: **I don't mind.⁹** I enjoy writing.

Philip: Well, maybe you should think about becoming a writer.

Robbie: Maybe I should.

Philip: You have lots of time to decide.

Robbie: That's **the worst¹⁰** part—making decisions.

Philip: You'll be OK. Good night, Son.

Robbie: Good night, Dad.

¹ anyway: I would like to know.
Use *anyway* with this meaning after an information question.

² What are you working on?
For information questions, the voice rises on the last stressed syllable, and then the voice falls.

What are you working on?

Prepositions such as *on* are not usually stressed in sentences. An exception is a preposition that is part of a two-word verb. For example, to *work out* a problem or to *work* a problem *out* means to try to find a solution. Since the preposition *out* is part of this two-word verb, *out* is stressed. Compare the intonation of the following question with the intonation of the example above.

What are you working out?

³ paper: newspaper

⁴ turn (it) in: give (it) to the teacher

⁵ What's it about? = What is the topic?

⁶ article: a piece of writing, usually for a newspaper or a magazine

⁷ scared: afraid; frightened

⁸ scary: frightening
This is the adjective form of the verb *to scare*.

⁹ I don't mind. = It doesn't bother me.

¹⁰ the worst
This is the superlative form of the adjective *bad*.
Use the superlative form to compare three or more things.
The comparative form of *bad* is *worse*.
Use the comparative form to compare two things.
    bad → worse → (the) worst

The next morning. Robbie is eating breakfast in the kitchen. Grandpa and Philip enter. They are singing the University of Michigan song.[11]

Grandpa &
Philip: "Hail to the victors valiant,
Hail to the conquering heroes,
Hail, Hail to Michigan,
The champions of the West!"

Philip: Ah, good morning, Robbie.

Robbie: Good morning, Dad.

Grandpa: How's my grandson?

Robbie: Fine, Grandpa. Fine! What's all the **cheering**[12] about? Did the University of Michigan win another football game?

Grandpa: Better than that. Tell him, Philip.

Philip: I just spoke with Charley Rafer.

Robbie: Who's Charley Rafer?

Philip: He's the **Dean of Admissions**[13] for the University of Michigan.

Grandpa: And **it turns out**[14] he's a **classmate**[15] of Philip's.

Philip: We were both on the tennis team.

Robbie: Great!

Philip: It *is* great. He's going to be in New York tomorrow to **interview**[16] **applicants**[17] for admission.

Grandpa: And he's agreed to **fit you into his schedule.**[18]

Robbie: But I may not want to go to Michigan.

Philip: It's one of **the best**[19] **schools**[20] in the country, Robbie. I studied medicine there. Your grandfather went to the **Engineering School**[21] there.

Robbie: I know that, but . . .

Grandpa: You said you wanted to be a doctor like your father.

Robbie: Not exactly.

Grandpa: You couldn't pick a finer medical school than Michigan.

Robbie: Yes, I know that.

11 University of Michigan song
Many universities have special songs for their sports teams.

MICHIGAN

12 cheering: shouting approval
You often *cheer* when you want a team to win a game.

13 Dean of Admissions: the person in charge of deciding which students may enter a school or university

14 it turns out: the interesting fact is

15 classmate: another student in your class

16 interview: to meet in order to ask questions

17 applicants: people who apply
A college *applicant* is a person who wants to study at a particular college.

18 fit (you) into his schedule: to find time to meet with (you)

19 the best
This is the superlative form of the adjective *good*.
The comparative form is *better*.
good → better → (the) best

20 schools
Here, *schools* means "universities."

21 Engineering School
A university often has many colleges, or *schools*, such as a law school, a medical school, and an engineering school.

Philip: Let's meet with Charley at the **university club.**[22] Ten o'clock tomorrow morning. It doesn't mean you're going to Michigan.

Grandpa: It doesn't mean you have to be a doctor. But the interview will be good experience for you.

Robbie: **In that case,**[23] it's OK. *[to Philip]* Dad, growing up means making *my* own decisions, doesn't it?

Philip: You're right, Robbie. But, **like your Grandpa suggested,**[24] have the interview.

Grandpa: And then make your own decision.

Robbie: That sounds fine.

Philip: I know it's sudden, Robbie, but this is an important opportunity. We'll **head**[25] down there first thing tomorrow morning. OK?

Robbie: Sure, Dad.

Philip: I want you to know something, Son. I'm . . . very proud of you.

Robbie: Thanks, Dad.

Philip: Well, I've got an appointment at the hospital. I'll see you all at dinnertime.

Robbie: Bye, Dad.

[Philip leaves.]

Grandpa: Is something still wrong, Robbie?

Robbie: I'll be OK.

Grandpa: Going away to college for the first time always makes one a little nervous.

Robbie: I guess so. I'll be OK. I just need time to think.

END OF ACT I

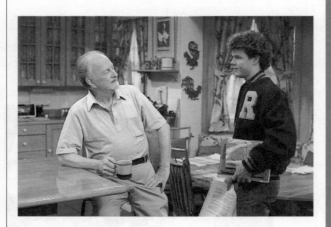

22 university club
Many universities have meeting places in different cities. The members of each of these clubs have graduated from the same school.

23 In that case . . . = If that's true . . .

24 like your Grandpa suggested
This is informal. The standard form is "as your Grandpa suggested."

25 head: to go in a certain direction

U.S. LIFE

In their last year of high school, students often apply to more than one college or **university**. A university is larger than a college. In fact, most universities have an undergraduate school and graduate schools in different fields such as law, engineering, and art.

Each college or university in the U.S. has its own requirements for admission. Most schools require students to take a standard entrance exam. To decide whether or not to accept a student, colleges or universities usually consider the test scores as well as the student's high-school grades. In addition, some schools require a personal interview.

Many students choose to go away from home and to live at college. Other students attend a state or local school and continue to live at home.

☞ YOUR TURN

- Do high-school students in your country usually apply to more than one college or university?
- Are high-school grades important for college admission? Is there a standard college entrance exam in your country?
- Do most students in your country leave home when they go to college?

ACT I **Activities**

Here are some activities to help you check your understanding of Act I.

AFTER GRADUATION

Why does Robbie feel scared and excited? Read each sentence below. <u>Underline</u> every sentence that gives a reason for Robbie's feeling scared and excited.

1. He's thinking about his future.
2. He doesn't want to go to college.
3. He may be leaving home.
4. His father says he must go to the University of Michigan.
5. He must make some decisions.
6. He cannot finish his article for the high-school newspaper.
7. He knows he's going to become a doctor.

THE UNIVERSITY OF MICHIGAN

Read each of the following statements. Circle *true* or *false* according to the information in Act I. If the sentence is false, change the underlined part, and rewrite the corrected sentence on the blank line.

1. The University of Michigan has a <u>football</u> team.　　TRUE　FALSE

   _____

2. Philip studied <u>medicine</u> there.　　TRUE　FALSE

   _____

3. Grandpa studied <u>medicine</u> there.　　TRUE　FALSE

   _____

4. Philip knows the <u>President</u> of the university.　TRUE　FALSE

   _____

5. Philip and Charley Rafer played <u>football</u> there.　　TRUE　FALSE

   _____

ACT II

The following morning. Robbie is sitting in the living room. He is waiting for Philip to take him to see Charley Rafer at the university club.

Philip: Sorry, Robbie. Sorry to be late this morning, but, well, we've still got some time for a cup of coffee. I can't wait to see my old pal Charley Rafer.

Robbie: Neither can I.

[They go into the kitchen.]

Philip: So you thought about it, huh?

Robbie: Yes, I have, Dad.

Philip: Well, I'm glad. I knew you'd realize that this interview could be an important experience for you.

Robbie: I **came to that conclusion.**[1]

Philip: That's very **wise,**[2] Robbie. Very wise. Now let's head off for the city and the university club.

Robbie: Thanks, Dad.

Philip: Thanks . . . for what?

Robbie: Thanks for **hearing me out.**[3] And . . .

Philip: And . . . ?

Robbie: And thanks for being such an understanding father.

Philip: Well, thank you, Robbie. Thank you.

In an office at the university club. Dean Rafer greets Philip and Robbie.

Dean: *[entering]* Philip Stewart! It's great to see you!

Philip: Charley Rafer—you look **as young as ever.**[4]

[They hug.]

Dean: You must be Robbie.

Robbie: Hi.

Philip: Yes, this is my **youngest**[5] son Robbie. Robbie, I want you to meet one of the best tennis players on the Michigan team—Charley Rafer.

Robbie: Nice to meet you, Dean Rafer.

Dean: Well, are you as good a tennis player as your dad?

[1] **came to that conclusion:** decided that

[2] **wise:** having intelligence from life's experiences

[3] **hearing me out:** listening to my point of view

[4] **as young as ever:** as young as you always looked
Use *as* + adjective + *as* to show equality.

[5] **youngest**
This is the superlative form of the adjective *young*. The comparative form is *younger*.
Philip should really say *my younger son* because he has only two sons. But he has three children, and he is probably thinking that Robbie is his youngest *child*.

Robbie:	No, I'm not very **good at**[6] it.
Philip:	**Frankly,**[7] neither was I. Charley was the star of the team.
Dean:	Yeah. Thanks. Well, how've you been, Philip?
Philip:	Oh, working too hard.
Dean:	**Doesn't show.**[8] How's Ellen?
Philip:	Fine, thank you. And how's Marge?
Dean:	She's still giving **the toughest**[9] English history exams in the school and loving every minute of it. And speaking of minutes, I have interviews until noon, so why don't we **get right to**[10] work?
Philip:	Can you have lunch with us later?
Dean:	I'd love to, Philip, but I'm afraid I can't. I'm only here two days, and I have interviews with twenty-six applicants.
Philip:	I understand. Well, thanks. I'll wait outside. *[to Robbie]* Good luck, Son. *[He leaves.]*
Dean:	Did you bring your **transcript**[11] from high school?
Robbie:	Yes, sir. Right here.
Dean:	Thank you. Please sit down. I see under "activities" that you've been writing for the school paper.
Robbie:	Yes, sir.
Dean:	What kinds of articles have you written?
Robbie:	All kinds—sports, **editorials,**[12] **theater reviews.**[13] You name it, I've written it.
Dean:	Hmmm. Well, have you ever thought of becoming a **journalist?**[14]
Robbie:	A professional writer? Not until recently.
Dean:	Michigan has a fine School of Journalism.
Robbie:	Yes, I know that.
Dean:	You seem to have some **reservations.**[15]
Robbie:	I'm a little uncertain.

[We see Philip nervously waiting outside the office. Dean Rafer has finished interviewing Robbie.]

Dean:	*[to Robbie]* It's been very nice talking to you.
Robbie:	Nice talking to you, sir.
Dean:	One piece of advice. The most important thing is for you to decide your own future.
Robbie:	Yes, sir. Good-bye, Dean Rafer.
Dean:	Good-bye, Robbie. Good luck.

END OF ACT II

[6] **good at:** talented

[7] **frankly:** honestly; truthfully

[8] **Doesn't show.** = It doesn't show.
Dean Rafer means that Philip doesn't look as if he's been working too hard. In other words, he thinks that Philip looks good.

[9] **the toughest:** the most difficult
This is the superlative form of the adjective *tough*.

[10] **get right to:** to start (something) immediately

[11] **transcript:** an official document listing a student's grades

[12] **editorials:** newspaper articles that give the editor's opinion about something in the news

[13] **theater reviews:** a piece of writing in a newspaper that tells about a play and gives the writer's opinion of it. Newspapers also include *reviews* of films, television programs, and books.

[14] **journalist:** a person who works to gather, write, edit, publish, or report the news; a reporter

[15] **reservations:** feelings of not being sure about something

U.S. LIFE

The most common college degree is a bachelor of arts, or a B.A., degree. This degree usually requires four years of study. During the first two years, a student often takes **liberal arts** courses to receive a general education. Liberal arts courses include the study of literature, languages, and history. Then, in the last two years of college, a student focuses on a major subject, his or her specialization.

☞ YOUR TURN

- Which college degrees are the most common in your country?
- In which year of college does a student usually begin to focus on a major subject?

ACT II

Activities

Here are some activities to help you check your understanding of Act II.

IT'S UP TO YOU

Complete the following sentences from Robbie's interview. If you wish, you may look back at the script for Act II.

> What kinds of _____ have you written?

> All kinds— _____, _____; _____.

> Well, have you ever thought of becoming a _____?

> A professional _____? Not until recently.

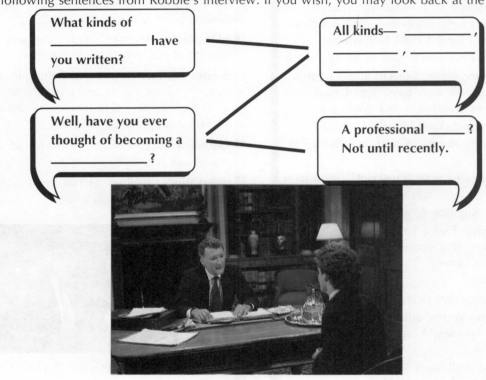

WORD SEARCH

Read the clues. Then find the words and circle them. The answers are written across or down. The first two answers are given.

CLUES

1. Robbie came to the *conclusion* that the interview could be an important experience for him.
2. Robbie thanked his father for *hearing* him out.
3. Philip said that Charley Rafer looked _____ young as ever.
4. Robbie told the dean that he wasn't very _____ at tennis.
5. Dean Rafer had a lot of interviews so he wanted to _____ right to work.
6. The dean asked Robbie for his high-school _____.
7. The dean saw that Robbie had some _____ about becoming a journalist.

```
C R P N H Y T H F M O D
E B O A C X R E F L E J
B G E T L N A A S F I O
V O T K H I N R L T W B
C O N C L U S I O N V S
R D P J O I C N S P E N
U S T I O G R G F I P N
C R O M P L I D O G J R
K I O X I T P M U I D D
S H I R A D T M J O S H
R E S E R V A T I O N S
B R I A N A P W L K M O
```

ACT III

On the patio of the Stewart's home later that day. Robbie is watering the flowers. He is speaking with his friend Mike about their interviews for college.

Mike: I had an interview today, too. I had a great interview with Admissions at **Columbia University.**[1]

Robbie: Really? What did they say? Will you get into the school?

Mike: Well, they didn't say anything for sure. *[joking]* But I figure that with my grades and with my personality, I'll have no problem.

Robbie: Columbia's a terrific school. What are you going to do?

Mike: Do? I don't know. I also applied to **NYU.**[2]

Robbie: You sound excited about Columbia. What's your problem, Mike?

Mike: **Indecision.**[3] Indecision. It's not easy, and this is an important decision we have to make. What about you? How was your interview with Michigan?

Robbie: The interview was fine.

Mike: It's a great college.

Robbie: It is. My father would like me to go there. He and my Grandpa both went there.

Mike: Great medical school, too.

Robbie: I know.

Mike: You can **follow in your father's footsteps.**[4]

Robbie: Ah! I'd like to follow in my own footsteps, Mike.

Mike: What do you want to study?

Robbie: I've been thinking. I think I want to study journalism to be a reporter—a newspaperman.

Mike: You do a pretty good job on the Riverdale High School paper.

Robbie: And I've been thinking about it a lot lately.

Mike: Have you discussed it with your parents?

Robbie: No. But I have to.

Mike: OK. Let's talk.

[They leave.]

[1] **Columbia University:** a private university in New York City

[2] **NYU:** New York University
This is another private university in New York City.

[3] **indecision:** not being able to decide, or choose

[4] **follow in your father's footsteps:** to become like your father
Here, Mike means that Robbie can be a doctor, like his father.

That night. Robbie is sitting in the living room of his home. Philip enters.

Philip: Hi, Son. Is everything all right?

Robbie: Hi, Dad. Everything's fine. I was just waiting for you to get home so we could talk.

Philip: Anything special you want to talk about?

Robbie: There *is,* Dad.

Philip: I'm listening.

Robbie: Well, I know you and Mom have **given up**[5] a lot to save money for my college **tuition.**[6]

Philip: We want you to go to college, Robbie.

Robbie: I know. I do.

Philip: But?

Robbie: Well, I've thought a lot about which college, and one of them is Columbia.

Philip: Columbia? Why Columbia?

Robbie: First, they have an excellent School of Journalism.

Philip: They do. And your friends are planning to go to Columbia?

Robbie: That's only part of it. It's complicated. I'll try to explain. Mike and I had a hamburger this afternoon, and we talked.

Philip: Yes?

Robbie: Well, we talked about a lot of things. He applied to Columbia, and his interview was very successful. He thinks he'll be **accepted,**[7] and he really wants to go there.

Philip: Dean Rafer called me today. He told me he was very **impressed**[8] with you.

Robbie: He's a nice man. He was very kind.

Philip: He told me you had some doubts about wanting to go to Michigan.

Robbie: Yes. I do. I'm just not sure about what I want to do.

Philip: That's OK.

Robbie: You understand?

Philip: Let me tell you something, Robbie. Something that might be surprising to you.

Robbie: What? Tell me.

Philip: Well, Grandpa wanted me to study engineering, like him. Well, I wasn't **clear**[9] about my future, but I knew engineering was not for me.

Robbie: What did you tell Grandpa?

[5] **given up:** sacrificed
Robbie means that his parents have not spent money for themselves in order to save money to pay for his college education.

[6] **tuition:** the cost of education at a college or private school

[7] **accepted:** permitted to enter

[8] **impressed:** having a positive opinion or feeling about someone or something

[9] **clear:** sure

Philip:	The truth.
Robbie:	Then you're not upset about my not wanting to go into medicine?
Philip:	I'm not upset at all. I'm just happy that we're able to talk about it.
Robbie:	I am too, Dad.
Philip:	I suppose you want to apply to Columbia.
Robbie:	Yes, but I also want to apply to several other colleges.
Philip:	I thought you wanted to go to Columbia.
Robbie:	Well, I might want to go to Columbia. But I might not. I just want to be able to make my own decision.
Philip:	You're **a real Stewart!**[10]
Robbie:	And if I think about it long enough, you never know . . .
Philip:	Never know what?
Robbie:	If I make my own decision, I might choose Michigan.
Philip:	Robbie, you're something! You know, when I was your age, I said exactly the same thing to Grandpa.

[They smile.]

END OF ACT III

[10] **a real Stewart:** like the other Stewarts
Here, Philip means that Robbie wants to make his own decisions. In this way, he is like other members of the Stewart family.

U.S. LIFE

There are both private and public colleges and universities in the United States. Private schools, like Columbia University and NYU, are more expensive than public institutions, which receive money from state or city governments.

More than 30% of young American adults attend college. There are about 3,000 institutions of higher education in the United States.

☞ YOUR TURN

• Is college tuition very expensive in your country?
• About what percent of your country's population attends college?
• About how many colleges or universities are there in your country?

ACT III

Activities

Here are some activities to help you check your understanding of this episode.

COMPARISONS

Study these rules for the comparison of adjectives. Then complete the exercises.

COMPARATIVE FORMS	SUPERLATIVE FORMS
Adjectives with one syllable	**Adjectives with one syllable**
Add *-er* to most adjectives.	Add *the* and *-est* to most adjectives.
EXAMPLE: young → young*er*	EXAMPLE: young → *the* young*est*
Adjectives with two syllables	**Adjectives with two syllables**
Use *more* or *less* before most adjectives.	Use *the most* or *the least* before most adjectives.
EXAMPLE: famous → *more* famous	EXAMPLE: famous → *the most* famous
Add *-er* to most adjectives that end in *y*.	Add *the* and *-est* to most adjectives that end in *y*.
(Change the *y* to *i* before adding *-er*)	(Change the *y* to *i* before adding *-est*.)
EXAMPLE: happy → happ*ier*	EXAMPLE: happy → *the* happ*iest*
Adjectives with three or more syllables	**Adjectives with three or more syllables**
Use *more* or *less* before the adjective.	Use *the most* or *the least* before the adjective.
EXAMPLE: expensive → *more* expensive	EXAMPLE: expensive → *the least* expensive

A. Use the information in the pictographs to complete each sentence. Use the correct form of the adjective in parentheses.

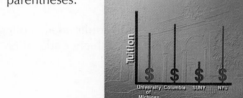

1. Michigan is _____ than Columbia. (*cheap*)
2. Columbia is _____ than SUNY at New Paltz. (*expensive*)
3. SUNY is _____ of the three schools. (*cheap*)
4. Columbia is _____ of the three. (*expensive*)

5. Columbia is _____ than Michigan. (*small*)
6. Columbia is _____ school for undergraduates. (*small*)
7. Michigan is _____ than SUNY. (*large*)
8. There are _____ students at SUNY than at Michigan. (*few*)

B. Look at the map to complete the two sentences. In each sentence, use the correct form of the adjective *close*.

1. Of all three schools, Columbia is _____ to Riverdale.
2. NYU is much _____ than SUNY.

C. Complete the paragraph. Use the correct form of each adjective in parentheses.

Choosing a college may be (*hard*) _____ decision that Robbie has ever faced. He thinks that he might be (*happy*) _____ at Columbia than at Michigan. Right now he's (*interested*) _____ in journalism than in medicine. And after talking to his father, he's feeling (*relaxed*) _____ than he did before. He thinks that Philip is (*wonderful*) _____ father in the world. Today, things seem (*clear*) _____ to Robbie than they seemed yesterday. Because now he knows it's all up to him!

"Smell the Flowers"

ACT I

ACT II

ACT III

In this episode, you will study . . .

VOCABULARY

approve	model
client [ˈklaiənt]	shy [ʃai] 照れ屋
staff 職員	embarrassing

GRAMMAR AND EXPRESSIONS

agreeing to do something for someone
telling time
talking about past customs: *used to; would*

PRONUNCIATION

ought to (awta)
used to (yoosta)

 U.S. LIFE

How do Americans feel about the free-enterprise system?

☞ **YOUR TURN**

Do women and men in your country have equal job opportunities?

Here is the complete script with study material for Episode 10. Use these materials before *or* after you watch.

ACT I

In Susan Stewart's office at Universe Toy Company in Manhattan. Susan is speaking with her assistant Sam.

Sam: Good morning, Susan.

Susan: Good morning, Sam. *[She enters her office.]* What's the schedule today?

Sam: *[He looks at the appointment book.]* Ten o'clock, telephone **FAO Schwarz**[1] about the new **twin baby dolls.**[2]

Susan: OK.

Sam: Telephone Mrs. Zaskey at the advertising agency.

Susan: I did that. Go on.

Sam: Eleven o'clock, **approve**[3] the **sketches**[4] for the toy **spaceship.**[5]

Susan: Where are they?

Sam: Right here.

Susan: Did you look at them?

Sam: Yes, I did.

Susan: What do you think of the spaceship?

Sam: I think the kids'll love it.

Susan: Would you show me the drawings, please?

[Sam gives a sketch of a toy spaceship to Susan.]

Susan: Huh. *[She examines the drawing.]*

A little later . . .

Susan: Now, what else is on the schedule today?

Sam: Well, at one o'clock you have a lunch appointment with Mr. Levine, the **client**[6] from the Toytown Stores.

[1] **FAO Schwarz:** a famous toy store in New York City

[2] **twin baby dolls:**

[3] **approve:** to say or write that someone's work is good; to say that something is OK

[4] **sketches:** simple drawings, without much detail

[5] **spaceship:**

[6] **client:** a customer

 U.S. LIFE

Susan is a vice-president of a toy company. Today, many American women are managers in the business world. More and more, women are holding stronger positions in large companies and in the professions, as doctors and lawyers, for example. In fact, in the U.S. today, almost half of all the people in the professions are women.

☞ **YOUR TURN**

In your country, is there equal opportunity for both women and men in business?

Susan:	Where?
Sam:	At Rossano's.
Susan:	Hmm. Anything else?
Sam:	At four o'clock, you have a meeting with the **production staff**[7] in the conference room.
Susan:	Make sure everybody is at that meeting.
Sam:	**Will do.**[8] At six you're meeting Mr. Ozawa.
Susan:	Oh, yes. Are his **models**[9] here?
Sam:	They're in my office.
Susan:	I'd like to see them.
Sam:	**Right.**[10]
Susan:	What else?

[Sam drops the appointment book and pencil on Susan's desk.]

Susan:	Come on, Sam . . .
Sam:	You work too hard, Susan. When was your last day off?
Susan:	Hmm. I can't remember.
Sam:	You really **ought to**[11] take some time off.
Susan:	**What for?**[12]
Sam:	To enjoy **the simple things in life . . .**[13]
Susan:	I know, Sam. Maybe soon.
Sam:	To **smell the flowers.**[14]
Susan:	Oh, wait a minute. What's today's date?
Sam:	Today is **the twelfth.**[15] Why?
Susan:	It seems to me I scheduled something else.
Sam:	There's nothing else in the appointment book.
Susan:	I'm sure I did. Oh, well, I'll probably remember it later.
Sam:	I hope it isn't important.
Susan:	Hmm. It's probably nothing. OK, let's get started. Would you call Priscilla Smith at FAO Schwarz, please?
Sam:	Right.

Later that morning . . .

Sam:	[He holds two model cars.] These are the models from the Japanese **film maker.**[16]
Susan:	Thank you. Just put them on my desk.
Sam:	And the new drawings for the toy spaceship.

7 production staff
A *staff* is a group of workers, or employees.
A *production staff* works together to make something.

8 Will do. = Sure, I'll do it.
This is an informal way to agree to do something.

9 models: small copies of objects
Before something is produced in large numbers, a *model* is usually made.

model cars

10 Right. = I'll do it.
This is another informal way to agree to do something. People also say *Right* to agree with someone's idea.

11 ought to: should
The informal pronunciation is *awta*.

12 What for? = Why?

13 the simple things in life
This phrase refers to simple things to enjoy, such as a good conversation, a beautiful sky, or a long walk.

14 Smell the flowers. = Take time to enjoy yourself.

15 the twelfth: the 12th day of the month
To refer to dates, use *ordinal numbers: first, second, third, fourth, fifth, sixth, seventh, eighth, ninth, tenth,* etc.

16 film maker: a person who makes movies
Alfred Hitchcock was a famous *film maker.*

Susan:	Wonderful. That was fast.
Sam:	We have a new artist. She's very talented.
Susan:	What time is it, anyway? My watch stopped.
Sam:	It's **eleven thirty**.[17]
Susan:	What time is my lunch date with Bill Levine?
Sam:	One o'clock.
Susan:	Remind me to leave at **twelve forty-five**.[18]
Sam:	Did you remember your other appointment for today?
Susan:	No, but **I have a feeling**[19] it's going to be too late when I do remember.

[Sam leaves Susan's office. A little later, he returns.]

Susan:	Yes, Sam?
Sam:	I just solved the mystery.
Susan:	What did I forget?
Sam:	You have some guests in the **reception room**.[20]
Susan:	What? Who?
Sam:	Mr. Harry Bennett and his daughter.
Susan:	I remember! Oh . . . Harry! I made a lunch date with him and his daughter weeks ago.
Sam:	Is he a client?
Susan:	He's a friend.
Sam:	Well he's here with his daughter to have lunch.
Susan:	I met her at Thanksgiving, and I promised to have lunch with both of them today.
Sam:	Yes, indeed. What are you going to do about your appointment with Mr. Levine?
Susan:	Any suggestions? *[She smiles at Sam.]* Oh!

END OF ACT I

[17] **eleven thirty:**

You may also say *half-past eleven* instead of *eleven thirty*.

[18] **twelve forty-five:**

You may also say *a quarter to one* instead of *twelve forty-five*.

[19] **I have a feeling . . .** = I think . . .

[20] **reception room:** a room in an office for receiving visitors or clients as they arrive

U.S. LIFE

Businesses in the United States are usually owned by people, not by the government. This is called **free enterprise.** Most Americans respect the idea of competition in business. Businesses must compete against each other for **profits,** the money that they earn. Many Americans believe that the free-enterprise system encourages equal opportunity. Part of the **American dream** is the idea that every citizen has a chance to own a business and become rich by working hard.

☞ YOUR TURN

• Does the free-enterprise system exist in your country?
• What does being successful mean to you?

ACT I — *Activities*

Here are some activities to help you check your understanding of Act I.

TIME

There is more than one way to refer to clock time. Study these examples. Then complete the exercises below.

 ten o'clock

 ten fifteen *or* a quarter after ten

 ten forty *or* twenty to eleven

 ten-oh-five *or* five after ten

 ten twenty *or* twenty after ten

 ten forty-five *or* a quarter to eleven

 ten ten *or* ten after ten

 ten thirty *or* half-past ten

 ten fifty *or* ten to eleven

Here is Susan's schedule for tomorrow afternoon:

```
2:00 ____
2:05 ____
2:10 ____
2:15 Meet with Mrs. Zaskey
2:20 ____
2:25 ____
2:30 ____
2:35 ____
2:40 ____
2:45 Production Meeting
2:50 ____
2:55 ____
3:00 ____

3:05 ____
3:10 ____
3:15 ____
3:20 Call Art Dept.
3:25 ____
3:30 Meet with Sam
3:35 ____
3:40 ____
3:45 Call Harry
3:50 ____
3:55 Review Budget
4:00 ____
```

A. Read the following paragraph. Then copy it on the lines below, but write each of the *times* in a different way. The first sentence is given.

At *two fifteen*, Susan will meet with Mrs. Zaskey. She will go to a production meeting at *two forty-five*. Susan must remember to call the art department, however, at *three twenty*. At *three thirty*, she will meet with Sam to discuss a new toy idea. She wants to call Harry at *three forty-five* to ask about his plans for the weekend. At *three fifty-five,* she has to review the budget for next year.

At a quarter after two, Susan will meet with Mrs. Zaskey.
____
____
____
____
____

B. Now imagine that Mrs. Zaskey will be five minutes late tomorrow. All of Susan's appointments will be five minutes later than they are on the schedule. Rewrite your paragraph, but make each time *five minutes later*. The first sentence is given.

At twenty after two (or two twenty), Susan will meet with Mrs. Zaskey.
____
____
____
____
____
____
____
____

ACT II

In the reception room of Susan's office. Susan greets Harry and Michelle.

Susan: Hi, Michelle. Hello, Harry. It's nice to see you again.

Michelle: Hello.

Harry: Hi, Susan. We have both been excited about seeing you and having lunch with you today. *[He hands Susan a bouquet of flowers.]* Michelle **picked these flowers out**[1] for you.

Michelle: Daddy, can we go soon?

Harry: We're going to go to lunch in a few minutes, honey.

Michelle: But I'm thirsty.

Harry: OK. You go out and get a drink of water at the fountain.

Susan: *[pointing]* The fountain is over there, Michelle. Near the Exit sign.

Michelle: Thank you.

Harry: Michelle is a little **shy.**[2]

Susan: I **used to**[3] be that way when I was her age. Harry, if Michelle doesn't want to go, we don't have to.

Harry: She'll be fine. Remember, I haven't dated anyone else since her mother died. This is a little difficult for her. Are you ready to go?

Susan: Yes. But could you wait one minute? I have a call to make. Would you excuse me? *[She goes into her office. Sam is there.]* Sam, get Mr. Levine at Toytown Stores on the telephone for me, please.

Sam: Right. *[He dials.]* Hello. Susan Stewart calling Mr. Levine, please. *[to Susan]* He's on the phone. *[He hands her the telephone.]*

Susan: Mr. Levine, Susan Stewart. I find myself in an **embarrassing**[4] situation. I made another lunch date for today and forgot to **enter**[5] it in my appointment book. Can you and I meet for drinks tomorrow? I'd really appreciate it . . . . Yes . . . . Thank you . . . . Tomorrow at five o'clock at **the Biltmore.**[6] I'll see you then. Thank you, Mr. Levine. *[She hangs up.]*

[1] **picked (these flowers) out:** chose (these flowers) *Pick out* is a two-word verb. You can also say, *picked out these flowers.*

[2] **shy:** not comfortable with other people; timid

[3] **used to**
Used to refers to past customs—repeated actions or conditions in the past. The informal pronunciation is *yoosta.*

[4] **embarrassing:** making you feel uncomfortable about yourself, often because you did something foolish

[5] **enter:** to write down
You use *enter* for business records, lists, and diaries.

[6] **the Biltmore:** a hotel in Manhattan

At the South Street Seaport later that afternoon.

Waiter: Welcome to the South Street Restaurant, folks. **What'll it be?**[7]

Harry: What do you recommend?

Waiter: Well, the **crab**[8] salad's always **a big hit.**[9]

Harry: Susan, would you like the crab salad?

Susan: I'd love the crab salad.

Harry: Michelle, would you like to try the crab salad, too?

Michelle: OK, Daddy.

Harry: We'll have the three crab salads and a **pitcher**[10] of **lemonade.**[11]

Waiter: Help yourself to celery and carrots and other vegetables.

Harry: *[to Susan]* We used to catch crabs.

Susan: Where was that?

Harry: We had a summer house on **Fire Island.**[12] Do you remember, Michelle?

Michelle: Sure. You and Mommy used to take me on the ferryboat.

Harry: Sometimes, at night, we **would go**[13] down to the beach and catch crabs, remember?

Michelle: With a piece of meat on a string!

Harry: Right. Well, I think I'm going to go get us all some vegetables.

[Harry leaves the table. The waiter arrives and sets down their food.]

Waiter: **There you go.**[14]

Susan: Thank you.

Waiter: And some **ice-cold**[15] lemonade.

Susan: Thank you.

Waiter: Enjoy it.

Susan: Michelle, can I help you with the lemonade?

[7] **What'll it be?** = What would you like? Waiters sometimes ask this question.

[8] **crab:**

[9] **a big hit:** very popular

[10] **pitcher:**

[11] **lemonade:** a cold drink made of lemon juice, water, and sugar

[12] **Fire Island:** a popular vacation spot off the south shore of Long Island, New York

[13] **would go:** used to go
Like *used to, would* refers to past customs.
With *would,* you must refer to a specific time period and frequency.

[14] **There you go.** = This is for you.
When putting food or drinks on a table, a waiter might also say *Here you are.*

[15] **ice-cold:** very cold

Michelle:	No, thank you. I'll wait for my father.
Susan:	Michelle, can we have a talk?
Michelle:	Sure.
Susan:	I know you miss your mother.
Michelle:	You do?
Susan:	Yes. And I'm not trying to take her place.
Michelle:	Then why are you and Daddy spending so much time together?
Susan:	Because we like each other. And right now, he needs a friend.
Michelle:	I'm his friend.
Susan:	I know you are.
Michelle:	Sometimes he's very sad.
Susan:	And so are you, I think.
Michelle:	Sometimes.
Susan:	I'd like to be your friend, too. Will you let me be your friend, Michelle? *[She offers her hand to Michelle. Michelle accepts it.]*
Harry:	*[He returns to the table.]* So, what were you two talking about?
Michelle:	Just **girl talk,**[16] Daddy. It's too hard to explain.
Harry:	You're probably right. Well, let's get started.

[They begin to eat.]

END OF ACT II

[16] **girl talk:** conversations between girls or women

South Street Seaport, New York City

ACT II Activities

Here are some activities to help you check your understanding of Act II.

"USED TO" AND "WOULD"

Study these rules about *used to* and *would*. Then complete the exercise below.

Use *used to* + a simple verb to refer to past customs. *Used to* may refer to a condition or to a repeated event.

EXAMPLES: Susan *used to be* shy. (a condition)

Michelle's parents *used to take* her on a ferryboat when they went to Fire Island every summer. (a repeated event)

With *used to*, it is not necessary to refer to a specific time period or frequency.

EXAMPLE: Michelle's parents *used to take* her on a ferryboat.

Use *would* + a simple verb to refer to past customs only when you refer to repeated events during a specific time period at a specific frequency. Do not use *would* to refer to past conditions.

EXAMPLE: When Susan was a young girl, her mother *would give* her piano lessons on Tuesday afternoons.

(specific time period: *When Susan was a young girl* specific frequency: *on Tuesday afternoons*)

Note that you may always use *used to* instead of *would* to refer to past customs.

EXAMPLE: When Susan was a young girl, her mother *used to give* her piano lessons on Tuesday afternoons.

Read the sentence with *used to* below each picture. In which sentence can you use *would* instead of *used to*? Circle *1, 2,* or *3.*

1. Susan *used to have* long hair, but now she doesn't.

2. When Harry was a boy, every summer he *used to get out* his fishing pole and go fishing.

3. Susan saw a picture of Harry when he was younger, and she said, "You *used to be* so handsome!"

TIME LINE

Michelle's feelings change in Act II. At the beginning of the act, she feels shy. Later, she feels comfortable. Read the sentences at the left. Write the letter of each sentence in the correct place on the time line to show the order of events at the seaport in Act II. The first answer is given

a. Harry talks about the summer house on Fire Island.

b. Harry orders lunch.

c. Susan tells Michelle that she wants to be her friend.

d. Harry leaves the table to get some vegetables.

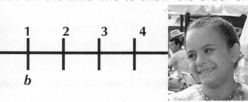

```
       1    2    3    4
───────┼────┼────┼────┼──────
       b
```

ACT III

At the South Street Seaport a little later. Susan, Harry, and Michelle are sightseeing.

[1] **It's so nice out.** = The weather is so beautiful. Here, *out* means "outside."

Susan: *[She looks at her watch.]* Oh, it's a quarter to four, and I have a production meeting at four.

Harry: I planned to take you for a ride in Central Park in a horse and carriage.

Susan: Harry, I'd love to, but I have work to do.

Harry: OK. We'll walk back to your office with you. **It's so nice out.**[1] I decided to forget about my accounting problems and just enjoy this beautiful spring day. Take the time, Susan.

Susan: I know I should, but . . . well, there are too many things to do.

Harry: I understand. I'll go for a ride with Michelle.

Susan: Right. Well, I had a really nice time.

Harry: So did I.

Michelle: So did I. I'm sorry you can't come with us, Susan.

Susan: So am I.

Harry: Bye-bye.

[He and Michelle start to leave.]

Susan: Harry! Michelle! Can you wait till I make a phone call?

Harry: Sure.

[Susan calls her office from a pay phone.]

Sam: Susan Stewart's office.

Susan: Sam, this is Susan.

Sam: Hi. How was lunch?

Susan: Fine.

Sam: You're late. The production department's waiting in the conference room.

Susan calls her office from a pay phone.

Susan: I know. Ask Paul Smith to **fill in for me.**[2] He knows everything about the production schedule, and **he can answer any questions.**[3]

Sam: Right.

Susan: Don't tell anyone, but I'm taking a little time to smell the flowers.

Sam: **Good for you.**[4] It'll be our secret.

Susan: But schedule another production meeting for tomorrow. I'll be back for my six o'clock appointment with Mr. Ozawa.

Sam: OK, Susan. And have a nice afternoon.

Susan: Thanks. *[She hangs up the phone and joins Harry and Michelle. They get into a taxicab.]*

Later, in Central Park. Harry, Susan, and Michelle are riding in a carriage.

Harry: She likes you.

Susan: I know. I like her.

Harry: How'd you do it?

Susan: We had a talk.

Harry: About what?

Susan: Life.

Harry: And what did you decide?

Susan: That's a secret . . . between us women.

[The carriage continues to ride through Central Park.]

END OF ACT III

[2] **fill in for me:** to take my place
To *fill in for* someone is to *do* someone's *job* for a short period of time.

[3] **He can answer any questions.** = If there are questions, he can answer them.

[4] **Good for you.** = I'm glad to hear it; congratulations!

 ## U.S. LIFE

The **South Street Seaport** and **Central Park** are two of New York City's **tourist attractions.** About 17 million tourists visit these places and other sites in the city each year. Central Park, in the center of Manhattan, is one of the largest public parks in the United States.

☞ YOUR TURN

- Which tourist attractions are popular in your city or town?
- Where might you go to "smell the flowers"?

ACT III

Activities

Here are some activities to help you check your understanding of this episode.

SMELL THE FLOWERS

Both Sam and Harry thought that Susan should "smell the flowers"—take time to enjoy herself. Complete the conversations below the pictures. Choose the correct phrases from the box.

the simple things in life	**take some time off**	**nice out**	**forget about**
many things to do	**beautiful spring day**	**What for**	

Sam: You really ought to _____ .
Susan: _____ ?
Sam: To enjoy _____ .

Harry: It's so _____ . I decided to _____ my accounting problems and just enjoy this _____ . Take the time, Susan.
Susan: I know I should, but . . . well, there are too _____ .

BUSINESS CROSSWORD

Use the clues to complete this crossword puzzle.

ACROSS

1. Money earned by a business
7. Time to meet
8. Write down in an appointment book
10. An informal way to agree to do something (2 words)
12. Please wait in the _____ room.

DOWN

2. _____-enterprise system
3. List of appointments
4. Business customer
5. Conference
6. Employees
7. Say you are satisfied with someone's work
9. Build a _____ before making the final product
11. Can you _____ in for me tomorrow?

"A Place of Our Own"

ACT I

In this episode, you will study . . .

VOCABULARY

lend 借給

borrow 借入　耗費

mortgage [mɔ:gidʒi]

salary

property 好招

stocks 股票　抵符 繁殖

bonds 繫的　記港

tradition

GRAMMAR AND EXPRESSIONS

nouns used as adjectives

sending regards 向松坛

ACT II

PRONUNCIATION

stressing auxiliaries in questions

运帮帮

U.S. LIFE

• What is the *American Dream*?
• Is it easy for people in the United States to own a home?

☞ YOUR TURN

• Which is more common in your country—owning a home or renting one?
• Is housing expensive in your city or town?

ACT III

Here is the complete script with study material for Episode 11. Use these materials before *or* after you watch.

ACT I

In the living room of the Stewarts' home in Riverdale. Marilyn is designing a dress. She stops for a while to talk to her mother-in-law Ellen.

Marilyn: Ellen, I'd like your opinion.

Ellen: About what?

Marilyn: Well, Richard and I feel that **with a baby coming**[1] we need to have our own place to live.

Ellen: Oh.

Marilyn: Well, what do you think about Richard and me looking for a small house or an apartment **at this point**[2] in our lives?

Ellen: We love having you here, and there is **room,**[3] and . . . and when the baby comes, the baby can stay in your room for a while.

Marilyn: Richard feels we need to find a small house.

Ellen: I remember when I was **pregnant**[4] with Richard. Philip and I were living with Grandma and Grandpa. Philip was a young doctor, and he kept talking about having a house of our own. It's natural.

Marilyn: What did you do?

Ellen: We looked at a lot of houses.

Marilyn: Did you find one?

Ellen: Oh, not at first. **We couldn't afford it.**[5] Grandpa wanted to **lend**[6] us the money to buy one, but Philip is too independent. He didn't want to **borrow**[7] any money.

Marilyn: Sounds like Richard.

Ellen: They're all **alike.**[8] Richard is a real Stewart. He's independent, and sometimes just **stubborn.**[9]

Marilyn: **When *did* you buy a house?** [10]

Ellen: After Richard was born. I was teaching music, and Philip was opening his first medical office.

Marilyn: Where was the house?

Ellen: Right here in Riverdale. Of course, it was a small house, but just right for us.

Marilyn: It's funny. History repeats itself. Now Richard and I are having a baby, and we probably won't be able to afford a house right away, either.

[1] **with a baby coming**
Marilyn means that she is going to have a baby.

[2] **at this point:** at this time

[3] **room:** enough space

[4] **pregnant:** going to have a baby

[5] **We couldn't afford it.** = We didn't have enough money to buy it.

[6] **lend:** to give something to someone with the understanding that the person will return it

[7] **borrow:** to take something from someone with the understanding that you will return it

[8] **alike:** similar

[9] **stubborn:** refusing to change (a belief or condition)

[10] **When *did* you buy a house?**
Marilyn emphasizes (stresses) the auxiliary *did*. You stress the auxiliary in a question to show that you are curious to know more about something in a conversation. Otherwise, the auxiliary in a question is not stressed.

Ellen:	Why don't you look at some houses, Marilyn?
Marilyn:	Good idea.
Ellen:	Look in the **real-estate section**[11] of Sunday's ***Times.***[12] You'll learn a lot.
Marilyn:	Maybe we should speak to a **real-estate agent**[13] about a house.
Ellen:	And a bank about a **mortgage.**[14]
Marilyn:	I'll talk to Richard about it. I think it's a good idea, Ellen. We *can* learn a lot by asking.
Ellen:	And if I can be of any help, let me know. As a matter of fact, my friend Virginia Martinelli is a real-estate agent.
Marilyn:	Good.
Ellen:	You won't believe this, but she sold us our first house and this one.
Marilyn:	Well, I'll tell Richard, and we'll go to see her. *[She looks at the dress she is designing.]* Do you think the skirt length is right, Ellen? Do you think it's too long?

Ellen:	I think the skirt is just right. Are you planning to attach a **train**[15] to it?
Marilyn:	No. No train. Just the dress. But I *am* going to make a **headpiece of lace.**[16]
Ellen:	That dress is gorgeous.
Marilyn:	Thanks, Ellen. And thanks for the advice about the house. I'll talk to Richard about it the minute he comes home.
Ellen:	And remember, we love having you here. There's no need to rush.

[They hug.]

END OF ACT I

11 real-estate section: the part of a newspaper that lists homes for sale

12 *Times*
This is a short name for the *New York Times*, a newspaper.

13 real-estate agent: someone who helps people find a house to buy

14 mortgage
To buy a house, most people borrow money from a bank or other institution that lends money. A *mortgage* is an agreement to pay back the money, usually during a period of fifteen to thirty years.

15 train: the back part of a long dress that touches the ground

16 headpiece of lace:

 U.S. LIFE

Since they got married, Marilyn and Richard have lived with Richard's parents. Now Marilyn and Richard would like to buy a place of their own. To own a home is part of the **American Dream**. Housing often costs Americans about 1/3 of the money they earn. Recently, the cost of housing in the United States has gone up faster than personal earnings. Therefore, many Americans cannot afford to buy a home of their own.

☞ YOUR TURN

- Do most people in your country own their homes or apartments?
- Is housing expensive in your city or town?

ACT I

Activities

Here are some activities to help you check your understanding of Act I.

A PLACE OF OUR OWN

Richard and Marilyn are thinking about buying a house. What things about *their* situation and Ellen and Philip's situation years ago are similar? Write *four* similar things on the blank lines. If necesary, you may look for the answers in the script for Act I.

1. _____

2. _____

3. _____

4. _____

ELLEN'S ADVICE

Ellen gives Marilyn some advice. Which of the following suggestions does she make to Marilyn? Check (✔) each of the ideas that Ellen gives her.

___ **1.** Look at some houses.

___ **2.** Save more money.

___ **3.** Find better jobs.

___ **4.** Look in the newspaper.

___ **5.** Go to a bank.

___ **6.** Call a real-estate agent.

___ **7.** Do not rush to buy a house.

___ **8.** Move far from the city.

ACT II

In a real-estate office in Riverdale. Marilyn and her husband Richard are speaking about homes with Virginia Martinelli, a real-estate agent.

Virginia: I remember your parents' first house very well. It was on Spring Avenue, near the park.

Richard: I grew up in that house.

Virginia: Yes, and you were such a cute baby.

Marilyn: I've seen pictures of him. He had **blond hair.**[1]

Virginia: I've been friendly with the Stewart family for a long time, so it's my pleasure to help you find a house now.

Richard: Well, we're not sure we can afford one.

Marilyn: But we'd like to find out about the possibilities.

Virginia: That's a good idea. I love your house on Linden Street. I sold your father that house seventeen years ago.

Marilyn: Really?

Richard: Yes, Mom was pregnant with Robbie then, and they needed the extra room.

Virginia: I hear *you're* expecting a baby, Mrs. Stewart.

Marilyn: Mmm-hmm. So we will be needing more room.

Virginia: Oh, so you don't need something immediately?

Richard: No. But in five or six months . . .

Marilyn: And time passes so quickly.

Virginia: Yes, it does. Well, when you called, you gave me enough information about your **salaries**[2] and your **savings.**[3] So I have a good idea about your **financial**[4] situation. Let me show you some pictures of houses.

Marilyn: With two bedrooms?

Virginia: Yes, I think I can show you some. Of course, they won't be in Riverdale. The cost of housing's too high for you here.

Richard: I haven't thought about living anywhere else. We've always lived in this area.

Marilyn: Where *should* we look for a house, Mrs. Martinelli?

[1] **blond hair:** yellow or yellow-brown hair
[2] **salaries**
Your *salary* is the money that you earn for your job.
[3] **savings:** money that you keep in a bank
[4] **financial:** referring to money

Virginia:	Well, we have an office in **Mount Kisco.**[5] It's a lovely area, and it's only about an hour's drive from here. *[She takes out a book of photos.]* Here. I have a book with photos of some homes in that area. Now, let's see. Here. This is a lovely **two-bedroom house**[6] **in your price range.**[7]
Marilyn:	It's pretty, but I prefer a **two-story home.**[8]
Richard:	I do, too. I don't care for a **ranch**[9] type.
Virginia:	OK. *[She turns the pages of the real-estate book.]* Oh, this is a wonderful house. I know it well. I sold it to the present owners.
Richard:	It looks wonderful.
Virginia:	This is a two-bedroom, **two-bath house.**[10] It has a **full basement,**[11] and it is on a **half-acre**[12] **lot.**[13] You can probably afford this one.
Marilyn:	I like this house.
Richard:	So do I.
Virginia:	And **the price is right.**[14] Would you like to go see it?
Richard:	Yes. We're planning to talk to someone at the bank next week. Perhaps we could see the house this weekend.
Virginia:	If someone doesn't buy it before then. But let's keep looking. Just to get an idea of some other possibilities.
Richard:	This is very helpful, Mrs. Martinelli.
Virginia:	Here. This is a wonderful example of Spanish-style architecture.
Richard:	Oh, I love the **roof tiles**[15] on a Spanish-style house.
Ellen:	It looks like the houses in Hollywood.
Virginia:	It's interesting. A house like this in Riverdale costs double the price. *[She turns the pages of the book.]* Oh my! Here's **a real buy.**[16] It's **a bargain.**[17] This house just **came on the market.**[18]
Marilyn:	It's quite lovely. Is it a two-bedroom house?

[5] **Mount Kisco:** a town to the north of New York City

[6] **two-bedroom house:** a house with two bedrooms
Do not use the plural *s* with nouns used as adjectives: *two-bedroom house*.

[7] **in your price range:** that you can afford

[8] **two-story home:** a house with two stories, or floors

two stories

[9] **ranch:** a house with one story

[10] **two-bath house:** a house with two bathrooms

[11] **full basement**
A *basement* is a part of the house below the ground, under the first story. A *full basement* is under the whole house.

[12] **half-acre:** a measure of land
One *acre* = 43,560 square feet.

[13] **lot:** an area of land to build on

[14] **The price is right.** = It's a good price.

[15] **roof tiles**

roof tiles

"This is a wonderful example of Spanish-style architecture."

[16] **a real buy;** [17] **a bargain**
These phrases mean "something with a good price."

[18] **came on the market:** became available, or ready to sell

Virginia: No. It has three bedrooms and three baths. I know the house. It has a **brand new**[19] kitchen. And a living room with a **twelve-foot ceiling.**[20] And there's a **two-car garage.**[21]

Richard: Then why don't we go look at this house, too?

Virginia: It's **a good investment.**[22]

Richard: Thank you, Mrs. Martinelli.

Marilyn: Thanks so much.

Virginia: My pleasure. **Give my best to your parents.**[23]

[Richard and Marilyn get up to leave.]

Virginia: Your father's a wonderful doctor, Richard. He took care of my daughter when she was a child. He's the best pediatrician in Westchester.

Richard: Thanks, Mrs. Martinelli, **I'll give them your regards.**[24]

Marilyn: We really appreciate your advice.

Virginia: I do think you should go see the houses and talk to the bank. Here. Let me give you some information **sheets**[25] about the houses. They're both very good buys.

Richard: Well, thanks so much for your help and your time, Mrs. Martinelli. *[to Marilyn]* We've got a lot to talk about.

Marilyn: Mmm-hmm. Thanks.

END OF ACT II

[19] **brand new:** made or bought very recently

[20] **twelve-foot ceiling:** a ceiling that is twelve feet high.

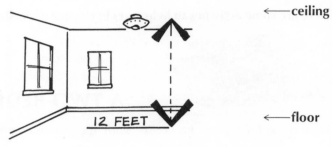

←ceiling

←floor

12 FEET

[21] **two-car garage:** a garage for two cars

[22] **a good investment**
If you buy something and later you can sell it for more money than you paid, then it is *a good investment.*

[23] **Give my best to your parents.** = Tell your parents that I give them my best wishes; say *hello* to your parents for me.

[24] **I'll give them your regards.** = I'll give them your best wishes; I'll say *hello* to them for you.

[25] **sheets:** pieces of paper

ACT II

Activities

Here are some activities to help you check your understanding of Act II.

Focus In

A TWO-BEDROOM HOUSE

Here is the floor plan of a house. Study the example at the right. Then do the exercises.

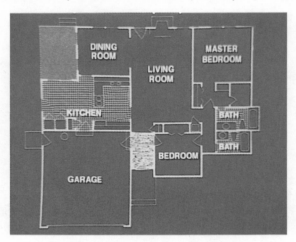

> You sometimes form an adjective with a number and a noun.
>
>   **number noun**
>
> **EXAMPLE:** This house has two bedrooms.
>
>   **adjective**
>
>   It's a two-bedroom house.
>
> Join the number and the noun with a hyphen (-). Do not use the plural *s* with the noun.

A. Complete the following paragraph. Choose the correct word in parentheses. Write the correct words on the blank lines.

When Richard was born, Philip and Ellen bought a small, two-_____
                                                             (story/stories)
house with two_____ . Philip and Ellen were both working, and
                  (bedroom/bedrooms)
they were able to afford the house. They had a thirty-_____mortgage. They
                                                      (year/years)
lived in that house for thirteen _____ ,until Robbie was born.
                                       (year/years)

B. What do you see in each picture? Use the nouns in the box to form phrases. Then write the correct phrase on the line under each picture. The first answer is given.

garage	home	acre	story	dollar	lot	car	foot	building	ceiling

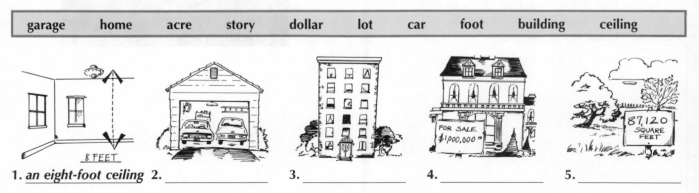

1. *an eight-foot ceiling* **2.** _____ **3.** _____ **4.** _____ **5.** _____

ACT III

In a bank in Riverdale. Marilyn and Richard are speaking with a loan officer[1] **about borrowing money to buy a house.**

Mr. Riley: How do you do?

Richard: Hello.

Mr. Riley: I'm Ralph Riley. *[He shakes Richard's hand.]*

Richard: I'm Richard Stewart, and this is my wife, Marilyn.

Mr. Riley: Pleased to meet you.

Marilyn: *[She shakes his hand.]* **Likewise,[2]** Mr. Riley.

Mr. Riley: Please, sit down. What can I do for you?

Richard: We'd like to discuss a mortgage.

Marilyn: For a house.

Mr. Riley: Fine. Are you buying a house or are you **refinancing[3]** your present home?

Richard: We're planning to buy a house.

Marilyn: And we'd like to find out about a mortgage.

Richard: We *are* customers of the bank. As a matter of fact, my whole family banks here.

Mr. Riley: I have some questions to ask. *[He writes on a form.]* Do you own your house or do you rent?

Richard: Neither. We live with my parents, Dr. and Mrs. Philip Stewart.

Mr. Riley: And how old are you?

Marilyn: I'm twenty-nine.

Richard: I'm thirty.

Mr. Riley: And, Mr. Stewart, what is your occupation?

Richard: I'm a **freelance[4]** photographer.

Mr. Riley: And, Mrs. Stewart, are you working?

Marilyn: Yes. I'm a designer, and I work in a boutique.

Mr. Riley: Did you bring any savings or salary information? Last year's **tax forms?[5]**

Richard: Yes. Here they are.

[1] loan officer
When you get a *loan* from a bank, the bank lends you money. If you want a loan, you speak to the bank's *loan officer.*

[2] likewise: I feel the same way.

[3] refinancing: getting a new mortgage

[4] freelance: working for yourself
Richard doesn't work for a company. He sells his photographs to different buyers.

[5] tax forms
Workers in the United States must pay a part of the money they earn to the United States government. This money is called *income tax.* The amount of this tax depends on the worker's total salary for the year. By April 15 of each year, workers must complete *tax forms* to send to the Internal Revenue Service. This is the agency of the U.S. government that collects taxes. Some state and city governments collect additional income taxes.

Mr. Riley: OK. What . . . what kind of house did you have in mind?

Richard: We're talking about buying a two-bedroom house in Mount Kisco. Here are the financial details on the house.

Mr. Riley: Thank you. *[He reads the details.]* Are you prepared to make a ten-percent **down payment?**[6]

Richard: Yes, we are.

Mr. Riley: Payments **over thirty years?**[7]

[Marilyn and Richard nod their heads.]

Richard: Yes.

Marilyn: Do you think we can get a loan?

Mr. Riley: Well, it depends. Do you own any other **property?**[8] Any **stocks**[9] or **bonds?**[10]

Richard: No.

Mr. Riley: I see. Then you don't have any **collateral.**[11] Perhaps you could get a **guarantor**[12]—someone to sign for the loan for you.

Richard: Why is that necessary?

Mr. Riley: Since you don't have enough **income,**[13] and you don't already own any property, the bank needs to be sure you can pay the mortgage every month. A guarantor is responsible for the loan if you can't **make the payments.**[14]

Richard: I see. Well, the *idea* of buying a house is exciting.

Marilyn: Thank you, Mr. Riley. We'll **read this over**[15] carefully.

Mr. Riley: Thank you.

Richard: Good-bye. Thanks.

Mr. Riley: Good-bye. And hope to see you soon.

Richard: I hope so, too.

[They all shake hands.]

Mr. Riley: **Take care.**[16]

Marilyn: Good-bye.

Later, on the patio of the Stewarts' home. Richard and Marilyn are speaking about their experience at the bank.

Richard: It all sounded so easy until they mentioned needing collateral or a guarantor.

Marilyn: We have no collateral.

Richard: And I don't think it's a good idea to ask Dad to sign as a guarantor. I don't feel right about it.

Marilyn: I understand your feelings about it, Richard.

6 down payment
When you get a mortgage for a house, you usually pay the bank part of the price of the home immediately. This is a *down payment*.

7 over (thirty years): during a period of (thirty years)

8 property: something you own, such as land or a house

9 stocks
If you buy *stocks* in a business, you own part of the company.

10 bonds
A business or the government may sell *bonds* to get money. If you buy a bond, the seller must pay back your money plus interest, or extra money, on a specific date.

11 collateral: property that a lender can take from you if you can't pay back a loan

12 guarantor: someone who agrees to pay back your loan if you cannot pay it

13 income: money that you earn

14 make the payments: to pay back the loan

15 Read (this) over. = Read (this) completely.

16 Take care. = Take care of yourself.
This is a common way to say good-bye.

Ellen:	*[She comes out to the patio with a tray of food.]* Now, tell me, what's the problem?
Marilyn:	We can get a loan from the bank if we can **put up**[17] some collateral.
Richard:	And we don't own anything to use as collateral.
Marilyn:	Or someone can sign with us as a guarantor.
Ellen:	Why don't you speak to Dad?
Richard:	No. If we buy a house, I want to be able to **handle**[18] it alone.
Ellen:	Everybody needs help sometimes, Richard.
Marilyn:	I understand Richard's feelings about it, Ellen.
Richard:	In two or three months, I'll have **an advance**[19] on my book and be able to **put more money down.**[20]
Marilyn:	What about the house in Mount Kisco? Somebody else'll buy it by then.
Richard:	Then there'll be other houses, Marilyn.
Ellen:	Richard has a point. You're just beginning to look.
Marilyn:	We're in no great rush. It's true.
Richard:	This has been a great learning experience for us, Marilyn. Talking to the real-estate agent. Looking at the houses. Talking to the loan officer at the bank.
Marilyn:	It *has* been a learning experience. That's true.
Ellen:	I think you're doing the right thing. Taking your time. Looking around. Especially with a **purchase**[21] of this kind. You're talking about a lot of money.
Marilyn:	We'll call Mrs. Martinelli and tell her to keep looking for us.
Richard:	And I'll call Mr. Riley at the bank and tell him we'll see him in a couple of months.
Ellen:	And if you ever need Dad or me to help you . . .
Marilyn:	We know.
Ellen:	You know **we'll be there for you.**[22]
Richard:	It's a Stewart **tradition.**[23] We're a family.

END OF ACT III

17 **put up:** to give
This two-word verb is usual with the word *collateral.*

18 **handle:** to deal with; be responsible for
Here, Richard means that he wants to be able to pay for a house by himself.

19 **an advance** *(noun)*: a payment by a publisher to an author before a book is published

20 **put more money down:** to give a larger *down payment*

21 **purchase:** something you buy

22 **We'll be there for you.** = You can ask us for help.

23 **tradition:** a custom

FOR YOUR INFORMATION

The most expensive private house ever built is **Hearst Castle**, in San Simeon, California. This house was built between the years 1922 and 1939 and cost more than $30 million. Hearst Castle has more than a hundred rooms. It also has a garage for 25 limousines. Today, this house is a popular tourist attraction in California.

ACT III

Activities

Here are some activities to help you check your understanding of this episode.

MORTGAGE APPLICATION

Complete only the shaded areas of Richard and Marilyn's mortgage application. You may look at the script for Act III to find the information.

MORTGAGE APPLICATION		INCOME	
PROPERTY		Monthly $	
Street address	City State Zip	Annual $	
		ASSETS	
BORROWER	**CO-BORROWER**	Stocks/Bonds ☐ Yes ☐ No	
Name *Richard Stewart* Age	Name *Marilyn Stewart* Age	If yes, cash value $	
Street address	Street address	Savings $	
City / State / Zip	City / State / Zip	Checking $	
Home phone number	Home phone number	**PROPERTY**	
Marital status ☐ Married ☐ Unmarried	Marital status ☐ Married ☐ Unmarried	Own ☐ Yes ☐ No Rent ☐ Yes ☐ No	
Education: _____ years completed	Education: _____ years completed	Do you own any other property? ☐ Yes ☐ No	
U.S. citizen ☐ Yes ☐ No	U.S. citizen ☐ Yes ☐ No	If yes, give address.	
Social Security #	Social Security #		
Employer	Employer	Total monthly expenses	
Address	Address	$	
Business phone number	Business phone number	**DEBT**	
Occupation:	Occupation:	Credit cards	
Years on this job _____ ☐ Self-employed	Years on this job _____ ☐ Self-employed	1. _____ $ _____ 2. _____ $ _____	
Do you have a guarantor? ☐ Yes ☐ No		3. _____ $ _____	
If yes, Name_____ Address_____ Home phone number_____		Loans 1. _____ $ _____ 2. _____ $ _____ 3. _____ $ _____	
Borrower's signature Date	Co-borrower's signature Date		

SCRAMBLED WORDS

A. Use the clue in parentheses to arrange the letters to form a word. The first answer is given.

1. D E L N   _L_ (E) _N_ _D_
(Can you _____ me five dollars until tomorrow?)

2. W O R O B R   __ __ ◯ __ __ __
(Can I _____ five dollars until tomorrow?)

3. T A M R O G E G   __ __ __ ◯ __ ◯ __ ◯
(To buy a house, you need a _____ from the bank.)

4. L A Y S A R ◯ __ ◯ ◯ __ __
(This job pays her a good _____.)

5. T O R R Y P E P   __ __ __ __ ◯ __ ◯ __
(He owns a lot of _____.)

B. Now arrange the letters in the circles in Activity A to form two new words. Use the clue in parentheses. (Mrs. Martinelli thinks a lot about _____ _____.)

EPISODE 12

"You're Tops"

ACT I

ACT II

ACT III

In this episode, you will study . . .

VOCABULARY

restless
confident
résumé
foreman
contractor

GRAMMAR AND EXPRESSIONS

adding emotion to statements (*yes/no* question form)
present perfect progressive verb tense

PRONUNCIATION

the sound of *t* between vowels (*a lot of*)

 ## U.S. LIFE

• How do older Americans spend their time?
• How does the U.S. government help senior citizens?

☞ YOUR TURN

Are there organizations of retired persons in your country?

Here is the complete script with study material for Episode 12. Use these materials before *or* after you watch.

ACT I

Grandpa, Malcolm Stewart, is in the living room of the Stewarts' home. He is waiting for his granddaughter Susan to come for dinner.

Grandpa: Is that you, Susan?

Susan: **It's me,**[1] Grandpa.

Grandpa: **Am I glad to see you!**[2]

Susan: And am I glad to see you! I am also glad to be here.

Grandpa: **How are things?**[3]

Susan: I **have been talking**[4] to a group of salesmen since ten this morning, and I'm **real**[5] exhausted.

Grandpa: Well, you look good. What's Harry doing tonight?

Susan: He and Michelle are visiting relatives in **New Jersey**[6] today.

Grandpa: The rest of our family went to the movies. So it's just you and me, Susan.

Susan: It's nice to be alone with you, Grandpa. We don't **get to**[7] see enough of each other.

Grandpa: Oh, I feel the same way, Susan. I miss seeing you. But to tell the truth, next time I'd like to go into the city and meet you there, instead of you coming here.

Susan: You don't need to do that, Grandpa.

Grandpa: Yeah, I do. I need to get out more. Well, I mean there's a lot to do around the house, and I love being here with the family, you know, but I'm **restless.**[8] Since I retired, I've got extra **time on my hands.**[9]

Susan: I understand, Grandpa.

Grandpa: I think you do. Frankly, I'd like to use my brain a little more.

[1] **It's me.**
This is informal. In formal English, *It is I* is correct. Most Americans use the informal form, as Susan does.

[2] **Am I glad to see you!** = I am so glad to see you! You can use the *yes/no* question form (a sentence beginning with an auxiliary and a subject) to add strong feeling, or emotion, to a statement.

[3] **How are things?** = How are you?

[4] **have been talking**
This is the *present perfect progressive* verb tense. Use this tense when an action or condition begins in the past and it continues until now *or* there is a present result now. Here, *feeling exhausted* is the present result.

[5] **real:** really
This is a nonstandard form. The standard word to use is *very*.

[6] **New Jersey:** a state near New York State

[7] **get to:** to have the opportunity to

[8] **restless:** not able to rest; feeling that you need to do something

[9] **time on my hands:** time with nothing to do

Susan: Grandpa, you have so much energy and so many years of experience. There are probably **a lot of**[10] places for you to work. Particularly in the construction field.

Grandpa: But at my age, I'm not looking for a full-time job. I'm retired. But I'm bored.

Susan: Well, there must be something. Maybe I can help.

Grandpa: Let's go into the kitchen, and maybe you can help me set the table.

Susan: Sounds good to me. What are we having?

Grandpa: I prepared **lamb chops,**[11] **mashed potatoes,**[12] and a **tossed green salad**[13] to begin with.

Susan: Grandpa, you are a terrific guy!

[They hug.]

A little later. Grandpa and Susan are eating dinner in the kitchen.

Susan: You're still thinking about something to do, aren't you? A job of some kind.

Grandpa: That's right. I've been thinking about it for weeks now. There must be some way to **put my mind to good use.**[14]

Susan: We'll find a solution. A positive solution to your finding a way to use that wonderful mind of yours.

END OF ACT I

10 a lot of
The *t* in *a lot of* is between two *o*'s. In American English, a *t* between two vowel sounds often sounds more like a *d*. This is one difference between American and British English pronunciation. In words like *better, water,* and *later,* there is a strong *t* sound in British English but not in American English.

11 lamb chops: a cut of meat from a lamb

lamb   lamb chops

12 mashed potatoes:

potatoes   mashed potatoes

13 tossed green salad:

14 put (my mind) to good use: to use (my intelligence) well

ACT I

Activities

Here are some activities to help you check your understanding of Act I.

PRESENT PERFECT PROGRESSIVE

Use the *present perfect progressive* verb tense (*have/has been* + *-ing* verb) to refer to an action or condition that begins in the past and continues until now. Look at the example below. Then complete the exercises.

Grandpa has been waiting for Susan since noon.

A. Complete each blank with the verb in parentheses. Use the *present perfect progressive* tense. The first answer is given.

1. Susan **has been working** hard, so she is glad to

             (work)

spend some time with Grandpa now.

2. Grandpa isn't working now. Since he moved to

Riverdale, he _____ home most

                 (stay)

of the time.

3. For the past few weeks, Grandpa

_____ about getting a job.

   (think)

4. Susan and Grandpa are finishing their dinner now.

Since she arrived at the Stewart home, she and

Grandpa _____ about his

             (talk)

problem; Susan _____ to think

               (try)

of a solution.

B. Read the paragraph. Circle the correct verb tense in the parentheses on each line. The first answer is given.

Grandpa (*is feeling* / *has been feeling*) very

                         1
restless now. He (*isn't feeling* / *hasn't been feeling*)

                             2
very useful in recent weeks. Since earlier today,
he (*is wondering* / *has been wondering*) about

                  3
what to do with all the time on his hands. He
(*isn't looking* / *hasn't been looking*) for a full-time

                  4
job right now. But for quite a while, he
(*is feeling* / *has been feeling*) bored. All day,

             5
he (*is having* / *has been having*) trouble thinking

             6
of a way to put his mind to good use.

ACT II

In Susan's office a few days later. Susan calls Sam, her assistant, into her office.

Susan: *[She speaks into the intercom.]* Sam, would you come in, please?

Sam: *[He walks into Susan's office. He is carrying a pad and pen.]* You sound like something's bothering you, Susan. The sketches for the cover of the new doll book?

Susan: That's not it. Please sit down.

¹ **matter:** a subject of discussion or concern
² **a big deal:** something very important
³ **runs:** directs
⁴ **founded:** began; established

Sam: Sure. *[He sits down.]*

Susan: I need your advice on a personal **matter,**¹ but it's not about me.

Sam: You need my advice on a personal matter, and it's not about you. OK.

Susan: It's about my grandfather.

Sam: What's the problem?

Susan: It won't sound like **a big deal,**² but it is. I had dinner with him Saturday, and he's very unhappy about not working.

Sam: I thought he was retired and pleased to be living with the family.

Susan: He is, but there's so much energy and talent in the man, and he doesn't get to use it.

Sam: But what can *I* do? What kind of advice are you looking for?

Susan: Simply this. John Marchetta **runs**³ this company.

Sam: He **founded**⁴ this company.

Susan: Right. John Marchetta gave me my start here six years ago, when I first graduated from college. He gave me the chance to use my talents and made me feel more **confident.**[5]

Sam: Right. Maybe he can do the same thing for your grandfather.

Susan: Or at least give him some advice.

Sam: Right. Then I've solved your problem. *[He laughs.]*

Susan: *[laughing]* I can always **depend on**[6] you, Sam.

Sam: I'm glad to help. Shall I call Mr. Marchetta for you?

Susan: No, no. I'll do that. Thanks. *[She picks up the phone to call Mr. Marchetta.]*

In John Marchetta's office later that day.

Marchetta: Now, how's the Stewart family?

Susan: Fine, thank you, Mr. Marchetta. Except for my grandfather.

Marchetta: What's wrong, Susan? What's wrong with him?

Susan: He needs to work. In fact, that is the reason why I'm here to see you. I know you're building a new factory, and I thought . . . maybe . . . my grandfather is so experienced in the **construction trade,**[7] he could be so **valuable.**[8]

Marchetta: Tell him to come and see me at ten o'clock tomorrow morning. I have an idea that may solve the problem for him and help a lot of other people.

Susan: Really,'Mr. Marchetta? Can I tell him that?

Marchetta: **Sure can.**[9] Ten o'clock in the morning. Here.

Susan: Oh, thank you!

END OF ACT II

[5] **confident:** sure of yourself; knowing what is good and bad for you

[6] **depend on:** to know (someone) will help

[7] **construction trade:** the business of building things

[8] **valuable:** useful
Susan pronounces this word as *val' yōo ə bəl*. Later, Mr. Marchetta says *val' yə bəl*. Both pronunciations are correct.

[9] **Sure can.** = You certainly can.
This is an informal expression.

ACT II *Activities*

Here are some activities to help you check your understanding of Act II.

WHAT'S THE MATTER?

Complete the following lines from Act II. Use the words or phrases from the box below. You may need to read Act II again to find the answers.

what can I do	depend on	bothering
advice	a big deal	matter
glad to help	wrong	solve the problem

1. Sam: You sound like something's _____ you, Susan.
2. Susan: I need your _____ on a personal _____, but it's not about me.

3. Susan: It won't sound like _____, but it is.
4. Sam: But _____?

5. Susan: I can always _____ you, Sam.
6. Sam: I'm _____.

7. Marchetta: What's _____, Susan?

8. Marchetta: I have an idea that may _____ for him and help a lot of other people.

BETWEEN THE LINES

According to the script for Act II, which of the following statements are true? Circle the number of each true statement.

1. Susan is very worried about the sketches for the new doll book.
2. Grandpa is pleased to be living with his family.
3. Grandpa now has many opportunities to use his talents.
4. Grandpa has a lot of energy.
5. John Marchetta has helped Susan's career.
6. Sam is Susan's boss.
7. Grandpa used to work for John Marchetta.

What's the matter?

ACT III

The next morning. Grandpa is in John Marchetta's office. He is waiting for Mr. Marchetta to enter.

Grandpa: Hi. I'm Malcolm Stewart.

Marchetta: John Marchetta. Sit down, sit down.

Grandpa: Susan has told me **a great deal**[1] about you. She says you're quite a man.

Marchetta: She says a lot of wonderful things about you too, Mr. Stewart.

Grandpa: That's always nice to hear, Mr. Marchetta.

Marchetta: Call me John. May I call you Malcolm?

[Grandpa nods.]

Marchetta: Let's **talk business.**[2]

Grandpa: **That's music to my ears.**[3]

Marchetta: I understand you used to be in the construction business.

Grandpa: Yup. Forty-three years. Here's a **brief**[4] description of forty-three years of **on-the-job training.**[5] *[He gives Mr. Marchetta his **résumé.**[6]]*

Marchetta: That is **some**[7] history! You're a valuable **asset,**[8] Malcolm. Very valuable.

Grandpa: Thank you. Yup. Forty-three years. Half that time in my own construction company. Big jobs—factories, **shopping malls.**[9] That kind of thing.

Marchetta: Then you retired.

Grandpa: Yes. After my wife died, and I felt I should spend more time with my children and grandchildren. I lived in Florida, and they lived in New York.

Marchetta: I understand. My daughter Cami lives in New York. I like being near her.

Grandpa: When I came here, I planned to take a few months off. Relax with the family and then look for some work. **Put my experience on the line** . . .[10] but, unfortunately, there isn't any work for a retired person my age.

Marchetta: Sometimes there is, and sometimes there isn't. Well, I'm involved with an organization, and we're trying to **resolve**[11] that problem.

[1] **a great deal:** a lot

[2] **talk business:** to talk *about* business
This is an idiom. Usually, the verb *talk* needs a preposition before an object.

[3] **That's music to my ears.** = It sounds great to me; that is what I want to hear.

[4] **brief:** short

[5] **on-the-job training:** experience while working

[6] **résumé:** a statement that gives a history of your work experience and education.

[7] **some:** a wonderful
This is an informal use.

[8] **asset:** a good thing to have

[9] **shopping malls:** groups of many stores with ways for people to walk and with a large area to park cars

[10] **put (my experience) on the line:** to test (my experience) by trying something

[11] **resolve:** to find an answer (to a problem)

Grandpa: What's that?

Marchetta: **TOPS.**[12] T-O-P-S—means Talented Older People's Society.

Grandpa: I'd like to be a member. How much are the **dues?**[13]

Marchetta: There are no dues. The organization serves **major**[14] companies in this city. Why? Because our members are men and women like you. Experienced, talented, retired. But our members want to go out there and use their talents. They want to work.

Grandpa: That is **fantastic,**[15] John!

Marchetta: I've got an idea for you, Malcolm. Just fill out this form for me. It'll only take a few minutes. Sit right here, and do it while I talk to my secretary. When I get back, we'll talk about my new factory. My company is a member of TOPS. So I try hard to find opportunities for people like you, Malcolm. And when I see an opportunity, I can act on it. Well, I can use your **brainpower**[16] on the job right now. Have you got time this morning to go over to the construction **site**[17] with me? I'd like to have you meet my **foreman**[18]—get some background on the job.

Grandpa: I've got plenty of time.

Marchetta: I'll be right back. We'll go over to the job site together.

[12] **TOPS**

Tops is an informal word that means "the best." But here, TOPS means **T**alented **O**lder **P**eople's **S**ociety. This is an example of an acronym. An *acronym* is a word that is formed from the first letters of two or more words.

[13] **dues:** the cost to be a member

[14] **major:** large and important

[15] **fantastic:** wonderful

[16] **brainpower:** mental ability

[17] **site:** location

[18] **foreman:** someone in charge of a group of workers, especially in a factory or in a construction business

 ## U.S. LIFE

There are many organizations of retired persons in the United States. Some of the members of these groups volunteer their time to help people in a particular kind of business. Other groups of retired persons work for educational, social, religious, or political causes.

☞ YOUR TURN

Are there organizations of retired persons in your country? If so, what do the members of these organizations do?

At the job site later that morning. Grandpa and Mr. Marchetta are speaking with Danny, the foreman of the construction project.

Danny: Malcolm, you worked on the Spaceport project?

Grandpa: My company was the **contractor.**[19] I built the theater there **with my own two hands,**[20] **practically.**[21]

Danny: I understand.

Marchetta: Well, I'm glad to see you two guys getting along so well because, Danny, Malcolm is on the TOPS team. He's going to be working with you for a while. His experience will be valuable to both of us.

Danny: **Welcome aboard,**[22] Malcolm!

Marchetta: I'm going back to my office. Give me a call later, Malcolm. I'll tell you the time and date of the next TOPS meeting. I'd like you to meet the group.

Grandpa: I will, John. And again—thanks.

Marchetta: No. . . thank *you.* And thank Susan. *[He leaves.]*

Grandpa: He's quite a man.

Danny: A real **inspiration**[23] for me.

Grandpa: OK, Danny. I know you didn't expect **to have me around,**[24] but I think I can **be of some help**[25] to you.

Danny: Let me tell you something, Malcolm. With your background and experience, I can learn something . . . and I do need some advice on a difficult problem. Let me show you this.

Grandpa: *[He looks at Danny's building plans.]* I don't want to give you a final opinion without studying these building plans more carefully. But a simple solution might be to move the **air-conditioning units**[26] instead of **redesigning**[27] the entire system. It might be simpler and less expensive.

Danny: You just **earned your weight in gold,**[28] Malcolm. Welcome aboard!

[19] **contractor:** a person or company that is paid to get materials and do construction work

[20] **with my own two hands:** without help; by myself

[21] **practically:** almost

[22] **Welcome aboard!** = Welcome to our group.

[23] **inspiration:** someone or something that strongly affects your action or thinking in a positive way

[24] **to have me around:** for me to be with you

[25] **be of some help:** to help a little

[26] **air-conditioning units:** large machines that cool the air

[27] **redesigning:** designing again

[28] **earned your weight in gold:** helped very much You can use this idiom when someone does great work.

In Susan's office that afternoon. Grandpa is telling Susan about his meeting with the foreman Danny.

Grandpa: It all happened so quickly! I can't believe it!

Susan: I'm glad Mr. Marchetta was so helpful.

Grandpa: He was more than helpful. He actually took me to meet his foreman.

Susan: I'm thrilled for you, Grandpa.

Grandpa: I don't know how to thank you, Susan. You're a wonderful granddaughter.

Susan: It's good to see you so happy.

Grandpa: I'll be at the construction site tomorrow. What are you doing tomorrow night?

Susan: I'm not doing anything. Why?

Grandpa: How about a date with your grandfather? I **owe**[29] you a good steak dinner.

Susan: I'll accept. Tomorrow night. You and me. Dinner. What time?

Grandpa: I'll pick you up here at seven. Is that OK?

Susan: I can't wait! And you can tell me all about your first full day **back on the job.**[30]

Grandpa: It's a deal!

[They shake hands and hug.]

END OF ACT III

[29] **owe:** need to pay back
[30] **back on the job:** returning to work

 ## U.S. LIFE

In the United States, the number of older people (senior citizens) in the population has been increasing. In 1900, 4% of the population was 65 or older. By the year 2030, about 16% of Americans will be senior citizens. The federal government offers help to older people. It gives them some money for food, housing, and health care.

☞ **YOUR TURN**

Does your nation's government offer special help to older people? If so, what does your government do for them?

ACT III

Activities

Here are some activities to help you check your understanding of this episode.

GRANDPA'S RÉSUMÉ

Choose the correct answer to each question about Grandpa's work experience. Circle *a, b,* or *c.* Use the script for Act III to help you.

1. How long did Grandpa say he was in the construction business?

   a. all his life

   b. forty-three years

   c. since his wife died

2. About how long did he say he had his own company?

   a. more than twenty-one years

   b. more than forty-three years

   c. for a few months

3. What kinds of construction jobs did he say he had?

   a. big

   b. small

   c. tiring

4. Which *didn't* he say he built?

   a. schools

   b. shopping malls

   c. factories

5. When did he retire?

   a. after he moved to New York

   b. after his wife died

   c. soon after he started his own company

RÉSUMÉ

MALCOLM STEWART

46 Linden Street
Riverdale, New York 10466
(212) 555-3090

...nce in Civil Engineering (B.S.E.), 1938. Magna Cum Laude. Un...
...n, Michigan. Recipient of Bertrand Hume Memorial Awa...

HOW DID THEY FEEL?

Complete each sentence with a word or phrase from the box. Write your answers on the blank lines.

1. Susan felt _____ after speaking to salesmen all day.

2. Grandpa felt _____ because he had so much time on his hands.

3. Sam felt _____ to help Susan with her problem.

4. Susan felt more _____ after Mr. Marchetta gave her a chance to use her talents.

| exhausted |
| restless |
| confident |
| glad |

"A Real Stewart"

ACT I

In this episode you will study . . .

VOCABULARY

nephew [ˈnevjuː]   height 高度
adorable   motto 格言·座右銘
generation 世代   crib 小床
weight 重   mature 成熟 到期 [məˈtjuɚ]
length [leŋθ]   diaper 尿布 [ˈdaiəpə]

GRAMMAR AND EXPRESSIONS

weights and measures
so and neither [ˈnaɪðɚ]
auxiliaries as verb substitutes
[ɔːgˈzɪljəri]

PRONUNCIATION

weight (wait)
length (lenth or lenkth)
height (hite)
auxiliaries

ACT II

U.S. LIFE

• What has the American government tried to do about the country's system of measurement?
• How many children are there in most American families?

ACT III

☞ YOUR TURN

• Which system of measurement does your country use?
• In your country, are there fewer children in families today than there were in the past?

Here is the complete script with study material for Episode 13. Use these materials before *or* after you watch.

ACT I

Ellen Stewart and her daughter Susan are in Richard and Marilyn's room. They are preparing the room for the arrival of Richard and Marilyn's new baby, Max.

Ellen: There's nothing more **joyous**[1] than the arrival of a new baby.

Susan: I am so excited, Mother! Just imagine— Marilyn and Richard must be thrilled! Oh, a new baby!

Ellen: Max . . . Max . . . Max. Oh, it's a sweet-sounding name for a sweet little boy. My first grandchild.

Susan: And my first **nephew.**[2] *[She looks at some photos of Max.]* Isn't he just **adorable?**[3] He looks a lot like you, Mom. He does.

Ellen: Do you think so? *[She looks at one of the photos.]* Well, I guess. He does look a lot like Richard, and I guess he looks a lot like me. Oh, he's got Richard's eyes, though.

Susan: I really want Harry and Michelle to see Max.

Ellen: When are they coming?

Susan: Tomorrow. Harry has an account to work on today. Yes, he does have Richard's eyes. Big blue eyes. The baby even looks at you like Richard does.

Ellen: Well, children usually **resemble**[4] their parents.

Susan: It's true. Michelle is a lot like Harry in so many ways. And she's shy with new people, just like he is.

Ellen: You really like Michelle, don't you?

Susan: Yes. **I'm very fond of her.**[5]

Ellen: And Harry, too? *[She looks at her watch.]*

Susan: Well . . .

Ellen: Uh, it's four-thirty. **Oh my!**[6] Marilyn and Richard will be home from the hospital **any minute,**[7] and we must prepare this room.

Susan: Where will we put all the presents?

Ellen: Well, let's take everything to the living room. Marilyn and Richard and the baby need the space. **It's crowded**[8] in here.

[1] **joyous:** happy

[2] **nephew**
Your *nephew* is the son of your brother or sister—or of your brother-in-law or sister-in-law. Your *niece* is the daughter of your brother or sister—or of your brother-in-law or sister-in-law.

[3] **adorable:** cute

[4] **resemble:** to look like

[5] **I'm very fond of her.** = I like her a lot.

[6] **Oh my!**
This expression shows surprise.

[7] **any minute:** very soon

[8] **It's crowded.** = There are too many things or people.

Grandpa: *[He enters.]* The welcome sign is up: "Welcome home, Max."

Ellen: Isn't it exciting, Grandpa?

Susan: Your first great-grandchild.

Grandpa: Yes. Yes, sir. A **great-grandchild.**[9] A great-grandson. Another **generation**[10] **to carry on the Stewart name.**[11]

Susan: I love you, Grandpa. *[She hugs him.]* You make me feel so proud to be part of our family.

Grandpa: And one day, you'll have your own family, and I'll be proud to be part of *it.*

Ellen: Now you understand my feelings, Susan. I'm Grandpa's daughter-in-law, but I feel like a Stewart. He's always made me feel like his own daughter.

Grandpa: Well, that's because you're so much like us—wonderful!

[They all laugh. Susan and Ellen kiss Grandpa.]

In the living room a little while later. Susan, Ellen, and Grandpa are wrapping some gifts for the new baby.

Susan: *[She walks into the living room and shows her mother that she has the wrapping paper for the baby's presents.]* Mom, got it. *[She sits down and looks at the baby album that she has bought for Richard and Marilyn.]* This will make a nice gift for Marilyn and Richard. They can keep a record of all of the important dates and information about Max's life here. Let's see. *[She takes a pen from the desk drawer and begins to write.]* Name: Max Stewart. *[to Ellen]* Does he have a middle name?

Ellen: No, just Max. I like that. No middle name. No middle **initial.**[12]

Grandpa: Like me. I'm Malcolm Stewart. Just Malcolm Stewart.

Susan: And Max has your initials, Grandpa: M.S.

Ellen: Uh, it must *mean something.*

Susan: **Weight:**[13] **eight pounds six ounces.**[14] *[She writes in the baby album.]*

[9] **great-grandchild:** a child of your grandchild

[10] **generation:** the new family members who are born at about the same time
Father, son, and grandson are three *generations.*

[11] **to carry on the Stewart name:** to use the Stewart name; to keep the Stewart name alive

[12] **initial:** the first letter of a name

[13] **weight:**
how heavy something or someone is. This is a noun form of the verb *weigh.* The pronunciation of *weight* is the same as *wait* [wāt].

[14] **eight pounds six ounces:** about 4 kilograms

Grandpa:	**Eight-six.**[15] Big boy! All the Stewart men were big.
Ellen:	Well, Robbie was eight pounds two ounces, and Richard was eight pounds three.
Susan:	And me?
Ellen:	Eight pounds six. You were big, just like Max.
Susan:	Eight pounds six, just like me. That's nice. **Length.**[16] Length?
Ellen:	Richard says Max is **twenty-one inches**[17] long.
Susan:	*[still writing]* Twenty-one inches. Is that tall or average or what?
Grandpa:	Tall. All the Stewart men are tall.
Ellen:	Well, Grandpa, you're about **five-nine**[18] or five-ten. **I wouldn't call that tall.**[19]
Grandpa:	I **take after**[20] my mother's family. They were . . . they were . . . they were **average.**[21]
Susan:	*[still writing]* Mother: Marilyn. Father: Richard. *[She turns the pages of the book.]* And lots of pages for Richard's photos of Max.
Grandpa:	Speaking of mother and of father—and speaking of Max—I hear the car. They're here!
Ellen:	Oh! Oh, quickly! Go, go, go!

[Ellen, Susan, and Grandpa rush to open the door. Marilyn, Richard, Philip, and Robbie enter the house. Marilyn is carrying Max.]

Ellen:	Let's see. Oh, welcome home. Oh, let her in. *[to Richard]* Wait with your pictures for a second. Come on, darlings. *[to the baby]* Sweetheart . . . . Sit down right here. *She walks with them into the living room.]*
Susan:	Oh, he's so cute! Oh, Marilyn!
Robbie:	Max looks just like Grandpa.
Grandpa:	**A real Stewart.**[22]
Marilyn:	I'm so happy to be home with my family—and with Max.

[The family continues to play with Max.]

END OF ACT I

[15] **eight-six:** eight pounds six ounces
You often shorten phrases for weight in this way.

[16] **length:** how long something is
This is the noun form of the adjective *long*. You refer to a baby's *length,* but you use *height* (the noun form of *high*) to refer to how tall older people are. In the word *length,* the *g* is silent, or it can be pronounced as *k.* The pronunciation of *height* is *hit.*

[17] **twenty-one inches:** about 53 centimeters

[18] **five-nine:** five feet nine inches
You often shorten phrases for height in this way.
Five feet nine inches is about 1 3/4 meters.

[19] **I wouldn't call that tall.** = I don't think that is very tall.

[20] **take after:** to be like

[21] **average:** normal
Here, *average* means not short and not tall.

[22] **a real Stewart**
The Stewarts often use this phrase. It means that one Stewart is like other members of the Stewart family.

 U.S. LIFE

Most countries use the **metric** system of measurement. This system uses *meters, grams,* and *liters.* The United States is one of the few nations that does not use this system in daily life. The government has tried to increase the use of the metric system in the United States. But many Americans have not liked the idea of changing their system of weights and measures.

☞ **YOUR TURN**

• Why do you think some Americans might not want to change to the metric system?

• Has your nation's government ever asked the people to change the way they think about something?

ACT I

Activities

Here are some activities to help you check your understanding of Act I.

WEIGHT AND MEASURES

Use the chart and the script for Act I to choose the correct answers to these questions. Circle *a* or *b*.

1. A new baby might weigh eight _____ .
   a. ounces   **b.** pounds
2. A new baby might be twenty _____ long.
   a. inches   **b.** feet
3. If a man or a woman weighs 300 pounds, he or she is probably _____ .
   a. fat   **b.** thin
4. If the height of an adult is four feet ten inches, he or she is _____ .
   a. tall   **b.** short
5. A car might travel forty _____ in one hour.
   a. yards   **b.** miles

WEIGHT	
1 ounce (oz.)	= 28 grams
1 pound (lb.)	= .45 kilograms

LENGTH AND DISTANCE	
1 inch (in.)	= 25 millimeters
1 foot (ft.)	= 30 centimeters
1 yard (yd.)	= .9 meters
1 mile (mi.)	= 1.6 kilometers

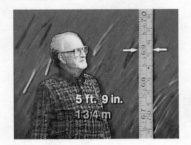

JUST LIKE US

Here are some statements, each one said by a member of the Stewart family. Who is talking—and who is he or she talking about? Complete each sentence with the correct name or names. If necessary, look back at the script for Act I to find the answers. The first answer is given.

1. "He looks a lot like you, Mom."
   **Susan** is comparing _**Max**_ to _**Ellen**_ .
2. "Oh, he's got Richard's eyes, though."
   _____ is comparing _____ to her son.
3. "And she's shy with new people, just like he is."
   _____ is comparing _____ to _____ .
4. "Well, that's because you're so much like us—wonderful!"
   _____ is comparing _____ to the rest of the Stewarts.
5. "You were big, just like Max."
   _____ is comparing _____ to Max.
6. "I take after my mother's family. They were . . . they were . . . they were average."
   _____ is comparing himself to the rest of his mother's family.
7. "Max looks just like Grandpa." _____ is comparing his nephew to his grandfather.

ACT II

Later that night. The family is in the living room. They are talking and wrapping gifts for the baby.

Susan: *[She looks at her watch and enters the living room.]* It's almost ten o'clock. I've got to go. Tomorrow is Monday, and work begins at eight in the morning for me. Oh, I'm so happy that Max is home. He's the sweetest little thing.

Ellen: I'll drive you to the station, dear. You can **catch**[1] the **ten-twenty train**[2] to **Grand Central Station.**[3]

Philip: I'll drive Susan, dear.

Ellen: Thank you, Philip. Then Grandpa, Robbie, and I can finish wrapping all these gifts.

Upstairs in Marilyn and Richard's room. Marilyn and Richard are watching Max sleep.

Richard: It's so good to have you home again . . . and to see Max asleep in his **bassinet**[4] at home with us.

Marilyn: To be with our family and all that Stewart **TLC.**[5]

Richard: TLC—tender loving care. That's our **motto.**[6]

Marilyn: Did you see the **washcloth**[7] and the **towels**[8] with the **teddy bears**[9] on them? Alexandra and the Molinas sent them for Max.

Richard: It was so kind of them. Now Max has come into everyone's life.

[1] **catch:** to have enough time to get

[2] **ten-twenty train:** the train that leaves at twenty minutes after ten

[3] **Grand Central Station:** a large train station in Manhattan

[4] **bassinet:**

[5] **TLC:** **t**ender **l**oving **c**are; kindness and love

[6] **motto:** a word, phrase, or sentence to express a belief or a rule to follow

[7] **washcloth:** a small cloth used for washing the face or body

[8] **towels:** cloths used for drying yourself after washing or bathing

[9] **teddy bears:**

FOR YOUR INFORMATION

The **teddy bear** was named after Teddy Roosevelt, the twenty-sixth President of the United States. Mr. Roosevelt was also a famous bear hunter.

Marilyn:	The house is so alive with him here. The welcome sign over the door. The boxes of presents. The M-A-X over his bassinet. Robbie put that there. *[She laughs.]* Susan's teddy bear. *[She holds it.]* So **cuddly.** [10] The beautiful **crib**[11] from Mom and Dad.
Richard:	Oh, and Grandpa's baseball glove. You know, it hung over my crib, too. And it hung over Robbie's crib.
Marilyn:	Part of Grandpa's magic?
Richard:	Oh, that's not all. It hung over Susan's crib.
Marilyn:	The same baseball glove?
Richard:	That's right. Grandpa hangs it there for good luck. He says it always brought him good luck on the baseball team. He believes it'll bring good luck to all the Stewart babies.
Marilyn:	And then he takes it back when Max is ready to use it?
Richard:	Yes, and **replaces**[12] it with a new glove so the old one will be ready for a new member of the Stewart family.
Marilyn:	Grandpa really loves his family, doesn't he? **So do I.**[13]
Richard:	And so do I.

[The baby begins to cry.]

Richard:	And so does Max.
Marilyn:	After he eats!

END OF ACT II

[10] **cuddly:** nice to hold close to you

[11] **crib:**

[12] **replaces:** puts a new one in place of an old one; substitutes

[13] **So do I.** = I do, too.
The negative form is *Neither do I* ("I don't, either").

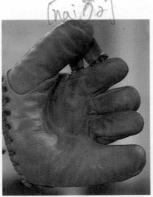

Grandpa's baseball glove

 U.S. LIFE

In American families today, there are fewer children than there were in past generations. Statistics show that the average American family now has one or two children.

☞ **YOUR TURN**

- In your country, about how many children are there in most families?
- Has the average number of children in families changed in recent years?

ACT II

Activities

Here are some activities to help you check your understanding of Act II.

SOMETHING IN COMMON

Study the use of *so* and *neither*. Then complete Activities *A* and *B*.

Use *so* and *neither* to express the same action or condition as in a previous statement. When you use these two words, you do not repeat the verb of the previous statement. But you always use an auxiliary (such as *will*) after *so* and *neither*. *So* refers to a positive verb; *neither* refers to a negative verb.

EXAMPLES: Marilyn will stay home now. So *will* Richard and Max. (Richard and Max *will stay* home now, too.)

Harry hasn't met Max. Neither *has* Michelle. (Michelle *hasn't met* Max, either.)

In positive statements with simple, -*s*, and past verb forms, there is no auxiliary. In these cases, use *do, does,* or *did* after *so* and *neither*.

• Use *do* to refer to a verb in a simple form (*love*):

Grandpa loves the Stewart family.

So ***do*** they. (Marilyn and Richard ***love*** the family, too.)

• Use *does* to refer to a verb in the -*s* form (*loves*):

Susan loves the Stewart family.

So ***does*** he. (Robbie ***loves*** the family, too.)

• Use *did* to refer to a verb in the past form (*loved*):

Ellen loved seeing Max.

So ***did*** he. (Philip ***loved*** seeing Max, too.)

A. Complete each of the following sentences with the correct word.

1. Harry will come tomorrow, and so _____ Michelle.
2. Marilyn is glad to be home, and so _____ Richard.
3. Alexandra didn't visit Max today, and neither _____ the Molinas.
4. Grandpa gave Max a gift, and so _____ Susan.
5. Susan feels a lot of love, and so _____ all the other Stewarts.

B. Complete each of the following sentences with the correct words. Use *so* or *neither* and the name or names in parentheses.

1. Grandpa doesn't have a middle name, and _____ . (*Max*)
2. Marilyn enjoys watching Max sleep, and _____ . (*Richard*)
3. Susan plans to visit Max tomorrow night, and _____ . (*Harry and Michelle*)

ACT III

In the Stewarts' living room the next evening. The family and Harry and Michelle are watching Marilyn unwrap the baby gifts.

Marilyn: Thanks, Michelle.

Michelle: I hope you like it.

Marilyn: Isn't this **baby outfit**[1] adorable? With his name on it—"Max." Thanks so much, Harry and Michelle.

Richard: We really appreciate it.

Harry: I'm glad you like it. Michelle picked it out.

Michelle: Yes. I told Daddy to pick blue ones. Blue is for boys, and pink is for girls.

Grandpa: And Max is some boy.

Richard: He's a real Stewart.

Grandpa: Right!

Ellen: That was so thoughtful of you, Michelle. Especially to pick it out in blue.

Susan: Would you like to see baby Max, Michelle?

Harry: Could she? Could we?

Michelle: Could I?

Marilyn: Take them upstairs, Susan. Harry and Michelle can watch Max sleeping.

Susan: Let's go.

Harry: Come on, Michelle. Before Max wakes up.

Marilyn: Will you please take this upstairs, Susan? *[She hands her a baby gift.]*

Susan: Uh-huh.

Marilyn: Thank you.

[Susan, Harry, and Michelle go upstairs.]

Philip: Michelle is very grown up for a ten-year-old, huh?

Ellen: She's smart and **sensitive**[2] for her age.

Grandpa: Growing up without a mother is difficult. **You**[3] **mature**[4] quickly.

[1] **baby outfit:** clothes for a baby

[2] **sensitive:** feeling emotions easily

[3] **you:** a person
Here, *you* is like the formal pronoun *one*.
In this case, it refers to anyone who grows up without a mother.

[4] **mature:** to grow; develop

Ellen: Susan's like a mother to Michelle. They have a good relationship. Do you think Susan and Harry will get married?

Robbie: Yeah. **You can count on it.**[5]

[They all laugh.]

Philip: I think so. Yes. They **get along so well.**[6]

Grandpa: I like him. He's good for Susan.

Ellen: He's a little quiet.

Richard: It's hard to do anything but listen in this family.

Ellen: **How can anybody get a word in**[7] around here?

Marilyn: You're right, Ellen.

Philip: Oh, really?

Richard: It's the way it should be. The Stewarts are the Stewarts!

Grandpa: They always were, and they always will be.

Richard: Right!

Grandpa: They've always got an opinion. Always got something to say.

Marilyn: And now there's Max Stewart, and if he talks as loudly as he cries, we're all **in for trouble.**[8]

Robbie: He's quiet now.

Marilyn: Mmm-hmm. That's because he's sleeping.

[5] **You can count on it.** = You can be sure about that.

[6] **get along so well:** have a good relationship

[7] **How can anybody get a word in . . . ?** = How can anyone have a chance to speak?
Ellen means that everyone in the family likes to talk a lot.

[8] **in for trouble:** going to have trouble

In Marilyn and Richard's room. Susan, Harry, and Michelle are watching Max as he sleeps.

Harry: He's really cute.

Susan: It's not necessary to whisper, Harry. A baby **gets used to voices.**[9]

Harry: I remember now. We always whispered when Michelle was born.

Michelle: And I didn't sleep well. Daddy told me. I never slept. And when I **did,**[10] I woke up when I heard someone speak.

Susan: I bet you were cute.

Harry: She sure was.

Michelle: Not as cute as Max. He's like a little doll.

[The baby starts to cry.]

Michelle: Oh, good. Now I can help **diaper**[11] him.

Susan: Let's get Marilyn. What do you do when he cries like that?

Harry: You pick him up. *[He and Susan laugh.]*

Susan: He's so little . . . so new. Let's call Marilyn.

Marilyn: *[entering]* Time for a feeding and time for a diapering. *[She puts the baby in his crib and looks at him.]* You're a real Stewart.

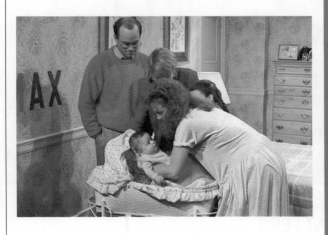

END OF ACT III

[9] **gets used to voices:** becomes accustomed to voices; hearing voices becomes familiar and natural

[10] **did**

Here, *did* replaces the verb *slept.* Auxiliaries often replace verbs, as in short answers like *Yes, I did.* When an auxiliary is a substitute for a verb, it is stressed; it is pronounced strongly. But when an auxiliary is used *with* a verb, as in a question, it is not usually stressed.

[11] **diaper** *(verb):* to change a baby's underclothes; to put a fresh diaper on a baby

A *diaper (noun)* is a soft cloth or paper folded between the legs and around the waist of a baby.

ACT III ▶ *Activities*

Here are some activities to help you check your understanding of this episode.

A REAL STEWART

Here is the Stewarts' family tree. What are the relationships among the people in the family? Refer to the family tree to complete the sentences below. Choose your answers from the box.

grandmother	grandfather	nephew	great-grandfather	grandson	great-grandson	aunt	uncle

1. Malcolm is
   Max's _____.

2. Susan is
   Max's _____.

3. Robbie is
   Max's _____.

4. Max is
   Malcolm's _____.

5. Max is
   Ellen's _____.

6. Max is
   Robbie's _____.

7. Ellen is
   Max's _____.

8. Philip is
   Max's _____.

FAMILY MATTERS

What did you learn from the family's conversation in Act III? On the line to the left of the number, put a check (✔) next to each *true* statement.

____ **1.** Michelle is excited about seeing Max.

____ **2.** Susan doesn't know Michelle very well.

____ **3.** Robbie thinks Susan and Harry will get married.

____ **4.** Philip thinks Susan and Harry will get married.

____ **5.** Ellen thinks Harry is a little quiet.

____ **6.** Richard thinks the Stewarts talk a lot.

____ **7.** Grandpa thinks it is good to tell your opinions.

____ **8.** Susan has a lot of experience with babies.

ANSWER KEY

Episode 1: "46 Linden Street"

Act I Activities

FAMILY ALBUM, U.S.A.
1. He's a photographer.
2. She's from Greece.
3. She works for a toy company.
4. She's Richard's wife.
5. He goes to high school.
6. Her name is Ellen.
7. He lives in Florida.
8. He's a doctor.

STORY LINES
a. 2   **b.** 5   **c.** 4   **d.** 1   **e.** 3

Act II Activities

"THANK YOU"
"YOU'RE WELCOME"
1. a
2. b
3. b
4. a

FIND THE NUMBERS
1. b
2. g
3. d
4. f
5. c
6. e
7. a

Act III Activities

INTRODUCTIONS
1. a, b   **2.** b, c   **3.** a, b   **4.** a, b

TRAVELING BAGS
The correct sequence is *a.*

Episode 2: "The Blind Date"

Act I Activities

FOLLOWING DIRECTIONS

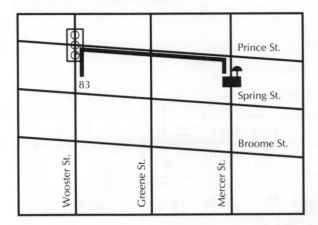

HARRY'S STEPS
1. g
2. b
3. a
4. c
5. e
6. d
7. f

CHOOSE YOUR WORDS
1. a
2. b
3. a
4. a

Act II Activities

OFFERING AND ORDERING
Here are some possible answers:
• I'd like a tuna salad sandwich.
• I'll have a cup of coffee.
• I'd like one scoop of vanilla ice cream.

GETTING TO KNOW HIM
A. accountant, numbers, daughter, Michelle, nine
B. (Your answers will give true information about yourself.)

ORDER, PLEASE
a. 3
b. 4
c. 5
d. 1
e. 2

Act III Activities

OCCUPATIONS
1. vendor
2. accountant
3. salesclerk
4. teacher
5. nurse
6. pilot

DATE LINE

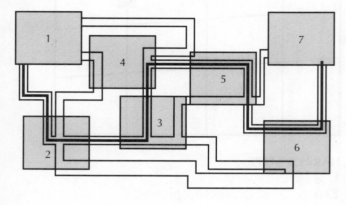

Episode 3: "Grandpa's Trunk"

Act I Activities

OPINIONS AND BELIEFS
1. a 2. b 3. a

LOOK WHO'S TALKING
Philip: 4
Ellen: 1
Marilyn: 5
Richard: 3
Robbie: 2

Act II Activities

PERSONAL INFORMATION
1. Pleased to meet you
2. Are you married
3. Where are you from
4. Congratulations
5. Do you have family in New York

NEXT STOP . . .
1. c 2. e 3. b 4. d 5. a

Act III Activities

THE FAMILY TREE
1. son
2. sister-in-law
3. grandson
4. brother
5. daughter
6. wife
7. husband
8. sister

WHAT DO YOU SAY?
1. Look me up
2. Small world
3. Congratulations
4. That's for sure
5. Take your time
6. Pleasant dreams
7. I can't wait
8. I've got it

Episode 4: "A Piece of Cake"

Act I Activities

IDIOMS IN ACTION
(Your answers will give true information about yourself.)

IN FACT
1. sixty minutes
2. tomorrow morning at ten o'clock
3. one hour
4. 555-8842
5. eight twenty
6. eight minutes

THE BET
Sentences 1 and 5 are correct.

Act II Activities

PRONUNCIATION
1. a 2. b 3. a 4. b

WHAT'S THE ORDER?
1. Jack takes Richard's blood pressure.
2. Jack asks Richard to take photos of the class.
3. The class begins.
4. Richard goes home.

AFTER CLASS
1. c 2. c 3. b

QUESTIONS AND ANSWERS
1. Jack, Richard, Nope
2. Richard, Jack, Anytime
3. Richard, Jack, Terrific

Act III Activities

"HOW MUCH" AND "HOW MANY"
1. How many
2. How much
3. How many
4. How many
5. How much
6. How many
7. How many

WORD SEARCH

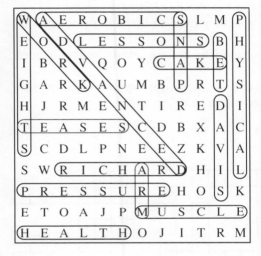

ANSWERS
1. Aerobics
2. Davis
3. work
4. physical
5. lessons
6. health
7. weights
8. muscle
9. cake
10. snap
11. teases
12. advanced
13. Richard
14. bet
15. pressure
16. arm

Episode 5: "The Right Magic"

Act I Activities

WEATHER
1. a
2. b
3. a
4. b
5. b

FISHING FOR IDEAS
Grandpa: c, a
Philip: b, d
Robbie: e

Act II Activities

DESCRIBING A SEQUENCE
arrived at the lake, used the right magic, caught a fish, cooked the fish, fell in the water

CATCH PHRASES
1. No way!
2. Sure. Come on.
3. You bet I have!
4. Burned, you mean.

Act III Activities

MAKING SUGGESTIONS
1. maybe, could
2. Maybe, can
3. Maybe, should
4. How about
5. maybe, should
6. Let's
7. what do you say
8. Why don't
9. How about

WHAT DO YOU SAY?
1. I've got to run
2. I'm very grateful
3. I'm thrilled
4. Come on
5. Nothing much
6. It'll be like old times
7. You bet

Episode 6: "Thanksgiving"

Act I Activities

POSSIBILITIES
1. Alexandra might call again.
2. Philip may have another cup of coffee.
3. Maybe Robbie will feel better soon.
4. Grandpa might talk to Robbie.
5. Maybe Alexandra will come by for dessert.

SPECIAL INGREDIENTS
1. apples
2. flour
3. sugar
4. butter
5. walnuts
6. cinnamon

THANKSGIVING MORNING
a. 5
b. 4
c. 2
d. 8
e. 1
f. 3
g. 6
h. 7

Act II Activities

LIKES AND DISLIKES
1. a
2. b
3. a
4. a
5. b
6. b

WHAT AND WHO
A. 1. c **2.** a **3.** d **4.** b
B. 1. b **2.** d **3.** c **4.** a

Act III Activities

THANKSGIVING

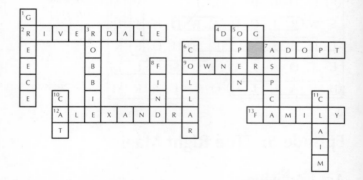

PREPOSITION DECISIONS
1. by, for
2. into
3. over
4. to
5. on

Episode 7: "Man's Best Friend"

Act I Activities

"SO" AND "SUCH"
1. such
2. so
3. so
4. such a
5. so, such a

A DIFFERENT "SO"
1. c
2. g
3. a
4. f
5. b
6. d
7. e

Act II Activities

PRONUNCIATION
1. The director at the A.S.P.C.A is very helpful.
2. The problem is they need to find the owner of the dog.
3. The hour is very late, but the animal shelter is open till nine.
4. Robbie has the idea to adopt Gemma if the owners (the Levinsons) don't call the office.

CROSSWORD

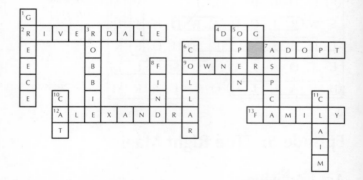

Act III Activities

PETS IN THE U.S.A.
1. bird
2. dog
3. fish
4. rabbit
5. cat

DIFFERENT REFERENCES
1. a
2. b
3. b
4. a
5. b
6. b

Episode 8: "You're Going to Be Fine"

Act I Activities

TALKING ABOUT HEALTH
1. I have a cold.
2. I have a stomachache.
3. I have a sore throat.
4. I have a headache.
5. I have a fever.

WHY? BECAUSE . . .
1. d
2. f
3. b
4. a
5. c
6. g
7. e

Act II Activities

PRONUNCIATION
1. ball
2. hat
3. sick
4. soon
5. made
6. song
7. pull
8. gone

CHARADES
1. fill   2. lip   3. S   4. two   5. heart

PHILIP	STEWART

Act III Activities

TAG QUESTIONS
A. 1. It hurts, doesn't it?
   2. It doesn't hurt that much, does it?
   3. I promised you a surprise, didn't I?
   4. And it wasn't just ice cream, was it?
   5. Your birthday is tomorrow isn't it?

B. 1. isn't it
   2. was he
   3. won't he
   4. doesn't she
   5. didn't they
   6. don't they
   7. did they
   8. wasn't he

Episode 9: "It's Up to You"

Act I Activities

AFTER GRADUATION
Sentences 1, 3, and 5 are correct.

THE UNIVERSITY OF MICHIGAN
1. TRUE
2. TRUE
3. FALSE: Grandpa studied engineering there.
4. FALSE: Philip knows the Dean of Admissions of the university.
5. FALSE: Philip and Charley Rafer played tennis there.

Act II Activities

IT'S UP TO YOU
Dean: What kinds of articles have you written?
Robbie: All kinds—sports, editorials, theater reviews.
Dean: Well, have you ever thought of becoming a journalist?
Robbie: A professional writer? Not until recently.

WORD SEARCH

ANSWERS
1. conclusion
2. hearing
3. as
4. good
5. get
6. transcript
7. reservations

Act III Activities

COMPARISONS
A. 1. cheaper
   2. more expensive
   3. the cheapest
   4. the most expensive
   5. smaller
   6. the smallest
   7. larger
   8. fewer

B. 1. the closest
   2. closer

C. the hardest, happier, more interested, more relaxed, the most wonderful, clearer

Episode 10: "Smell the Flowers"

Act I Activities

TIME
A. At *a quarter after two,* Susan will meet with Mrs. Zaskey. She will go to a production meeting at *a quarter to three.* Susan must remember to call the art department, however, at *twenty after three.* At *half-past three,* she will meet with Sam to discuss a new toy idea. She wants to call Harry at *a quarter to four* to ask about his plans for the weekend. At *five to four,* she has to review the budget for next year.

B. At *twenty after two* (or *two twenty*), Susan will meet with Mrs. Zaskey. She will go to a production meeting at *ten to three* (or *two fifty*). Susan must remember to call the art department, however, at *twenty-five after three* (or *three twenty-five*). At *twenty-five to four* (or *three thirty-five*), she will meet with Sam to discuss a new toy idea. She wants to call Harry at *ten to four* (or *three fifty*) to ask about his plans for the weekend. At *four o'clock,* she has to review the budget for next year.

Act II Activities

"USED TO" AND "WOULD"
Sentence 2 is correct.

TIME LINE
1. b   **2.** a   **3.** d   **4.** c

Act III Activities

SMELL THE FLOWERS
Sam: You really ought to take some time off.
Susan: What for?
Sam: To enjoy the simple things in life.

Harry: It's so nice out. I decided to forget about my accounting problems and just enjoy this beautiful spring day. Take the time, Susan.
Susan: I know I should, but . . . well, there are too many things to do.

BUSINESS CROSSWORD

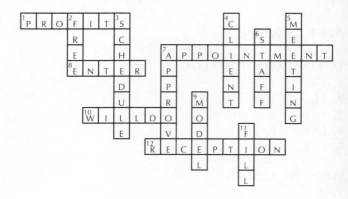

Episode 11: "A Place of Our Own"

Act I Activities

A PLACE OF OUR OWN
1. Marilyn is pregnant, and so was Ellen.
2. Richard doesn't want to borrow money from his father to buy a house, and neither did Philip.
3. Richard and Marilyn probably won't be able to afford a house, and neither could Philip and Ellen at first.
4. Marilyn and Richard will speak with the same real-estate agent that Philip and Ellen spoke with.
        (Other answers are possible.)

ELLEN'S ADVICE
Sentences 1, 4, 5, 6, and 7 are correct.

Act II Activities

A TWO-BEDROOM HOUSE
A. story, bedrooms, year, years
B. 1. an eight-foot ceiling
     2. a two-car garage
     3. a six-story building
     4. a million-dollar home
     5. a one-acre lot

Act III Activities

MORTGAGE APPLICATION
City: Riverdale
Richard
Age: 30
Marital Status: Married
Occupation: Freelance photographer

Marilyn
Age: 29
Marital Status: Married
Occupation: Designer and Salesclerk

Guarantor: No
Stocks/Bonds: No

Property
Own: No
Rent: No
Other property: No

SCRAMBLED WORDS
A. 1. LEND
   2. BORROW
   3. MORTGAGE
   4. SALARY
   5. PROPERTY
B. REAL ESTATE

Episode 12: "You're Tops"

Act I Activities

PRESENT PERFECT PROGRESSIVE
A. 1. has been working
   2. has been staying
   3. has been thinking
   4. have been talking
   5. has been trying

B. 1. is feeling
   2. hasn't been feeling
   3. has been wondering
   4. isn't looking
   5. has been feeling
   6. has been having

Act II Activities

WHAT'S THE MATTER?
1. bothering
2. advice, matter
3. a big deal
4. what can I do
5. depend on
6. glad to help
7. wrong
8. solve the problem

BETWEEN THE LINES
Sentences 2, 4, and 5 are correct.

Act III Activities

GRANDPA'S RÉSUMÉ
1. b 2. a 3. a 4. a 5. b

HOW DID THEY FEEL?
1. exhausted
2. restless
3. glad
4. confident

Episode 13: "A Real Stewart"

Act I Activities

WEIGHTS AND MEASURES
1. b 2. a 3. a 4. b 5. b

JUST LIKE US
1. Susan is comparing Max to Ellen.
2. Ellen is comparing Max to her son.
3. Susan is comparing Michelle to Harry.
4. Grandpa is comparing Ellen to the rest of the Stewarts.
5. Ellen is comparing Susan to Max.
6. Grandpa is comparing himself to the rest of his mother's family.
7. Robbie is comparing his nephew to his grandfather.

Act II Activities

SOMETHING IN COMMON
A. 1. will   B. 1. neither does Max
   2. is   2. so does Richard
   3. did   3. so do Harry and Michelle
   4. did
   5. do

Act III Activities

A REAL STEWART
1. great-grandfather   5. grandson
2. aunt   6. nephew
3. uncle   7. grandmother
4. great-grandson   8. grandfather

FAMILY MATTERS
Sentences 1, 3, 4, 5, 6, and 7 are correct.

USEFUL VOCABULARY AND EXPRESSIONS

The number after each word indicates the episode in which the word or expression first appears.

adj = adjective; aux = auxiliary; n = noun; v = verb

A

a bargain (11)
a big deal (12)
a big hit (10)
a day off (3)
a good investment (11)
a great deal (12)
a lot of (12)
a piece of cake (4)
a real buy (11)
accepted (9)
adopt (7)
adorable (13)
adult (7)
advance [n] (11)
advanced [adj] (4)
aerobics (4)
affection (7)
afford (11)
After you. (2)
air-conditioning (12)
aisle (3)
alike (11)
all (5)
all over the (house) (3)
Am I (glad to see you)! (12)
Amtrak (3)
anniversary (3)
any minute (13)
Anytime. [My pleasure.] (1)
Anytime. [You decide.] (4)
anyway [to mean something isn't important] (5)
anyway [to use after an information question] (9)
apologize (2)
applicants (9)
appreciate (your help) (1)
approve (10)
arguing (8)
article (9)
As a matter of fact . . . (2)
as (young) as ever (9)
asset (12)
at this point (11)
average (13)

B

baby-sitter (2)
back on the job (12)
bacon (5)
bags (3)

balloon (6)
bands (6)
barely (4)
barking (7)
bassinet (13)
be back (7)
be of some help (12)
beeper (5)
before eating (5)
belongings (3)
bet [v] [n] (4)
blanket (5)
blocks (2)
blond hair (11)
bonds (11)
bonsai tree (2)
borrow (11)
boutique (1)
brainpower (12)
branches (7)
brand new (11)
bridges (3)
brief (12)
brings back memories (3)
burned (5)
by [next to] (3)
by [to that place] (7)
by himself (3)
by plane (3)
By the way . . . (1)
by train (3)
Bye. (1)

C

cabinet (6)
California (1)
call (her) right back (6)
came on the market (11)
came to that conclusion (9)
can tell (7)
Can you do me a favor? (6)
can't wait (3)
canvas bag (1)
catch (13)
change (6)
charades (8)
cheer you up (7)
cheering (9)
chef (5)
chef's salad (7)
children's ward (5)

cinnamon (6)
claim (7)
classmate (9)
clear (9)
client (10)
close [adj] (2)
cloudy (5)
clowns (6)
colds (8)
collar (7)
collateral (11)
Columbia University (9)
come by (6)
Come on. [Do it now.] (5)
come on [to begin] (6)
come on [not to act like that] (8)
come up with (8)
coming up (8)
confident (12)
Congratulations! (3)
construction company (3)
construction trade (12)
contractor (12)
could (4)
CPA (2)
crab (10)
crib (13)
crispy (5)
crowded (13)
cuddle [v] (7)
cuddly [adj] (13)
cute (7)

D

date (2)
deal (8)
Dean of Admissions (9)
delayed (3)
depend on (12)
dessert (1)
destination (3)
diaper [n] [v] (13)
did [aux] (13)
different than (4)
disappointed (3)
do [really] (1)
do [can or should] (7)
do [will] (8)
don't mind (9)
Don't you . . . ? (5)
down payment (11)
dues (12)

E

earned (your) weight in gold (12)
Easy does it. (5)
editorials (9)
embarrassing (10)
emergency (5)
encouraging (6)
engineering school (9)
enough for an army (5)
enter (10)
entire (4)
ever (7)
exchange student (1)
excited (3)
Excuse me. [to get someone's attention] (1)
Excuse me. [to say before you walk away from someone] (1)
Excuse the (mess). (2)
exhausted (4)

F

family background (7)
family tree (3)
fantastic (12)
fashion show (2)
fellas (3)
fill in for (me) (10)
fill out (7)
film maker (10)
financial (11)
firm (2)
fit (you) into (his) schedule (9)
float (6)
folks (7)
follow in (your father's) footsteps (9)
fond of (13)
fooling (8)
foot [measurement] (13)
foreman (12)
forty-five [time] (1)
founded (12)
frankly (9)
freelance (11)
fried eggs (5)
frozen fish (5)
full basement (11)
fun (2)

G

gang (8)
generation (13)
get [to become] (7)
get [to take] (7)
get along (so well) (13)
get on (3)
get over it (6)
get right to (9)
get to [to go to immediately] (5)
get to [to have the opportunity] (12)
get to work (6)
gets used to (13)
girl talk (10)
Give my best to . . . (11)
give (someone's) regards (11)
give thanks (6)
given up (9)
go [continue] (4)
go along with (6)
going on (8)
going to (2)
good at (9)
Good for you. (10)
got [understand] (8)
graduation (3)
Grand Central Station (13)
grateful (5)
great-grandchild (13)
Greece (1)
grouchy (6)
guarantor (11)

H

half-acre (11)
hand (5)
handle (11)
handling (8)
hangers (3)
hard to resist (7)
harvest (6)
have (+ past participle) (7)
have a feeling (10)
Have a safe trip home. (2)
have been (+ -ing verb) (12)
have got (it) [have an idea] (3)
have got to (+ simple verb) (1)
head [v] (9)
hearing (me) out (9)
help (+ simple verb) (6)

Here they are. (1)
Here we go. (5)
Hey. (1)
Hi, there! (5)
Hispanic (1)
honey (3)
Hope to see you again. (2)
hot dog (2)
How (+ adj) ! (3)
How about . . . ? [to offer food] (2)
How about . . . ? [to suggest doing something] (5)
How are things? (12)
How do you do? (1)
How much . . . ? (4)
How (are) you doing? (8)
Huh? (4)

I

I'd like . . . (2)
I'll have . . . (2)
I'm. . . [to introduce yourself] (1)
ice-cold (10)
ID (7)
ideal (4)
if (7)
impressed (9)
in for trouble (13)
in great shape (4)
in place (4)
In that case . . . (9)
in that spirit (6)
in (your) price range (11)
inches (13)
income (11)
indecision (9)
infected (8)
ingredients (6)
initial (13)
inspiration (12)
intercom (2)
interview (9)
Is that it? (7)
Is this seat taken? (3)
It is possible that . . . (6)
It was a pleasure meeting you. (1)
It was nice meeting you. (1)
It'll be like old times. (5)
It's a snap. (4)
It's nice to meet you. (1)

J

jogging (4)

join in (8)
journalist (9)
joyous (13)
junior high school (3)
just (2)

K

kidding (4)
kids (3)

L

lady (3)
lamb chops (12)
last [v] (4)
lemonade (10)
lend (11)
length (13)
Let's . . .(5)
likewise (11)
loan officer (11)
lodge (5)
look forward to (6)
Look (us) up. (3)
lost-and-found (office) (1)
lot (11)

M

ma'am (2)
major (12)
Make a (left) turn. (2)
make the payments (11)
man's best friend (7)
mashed potatoes (12)
matter (12)
mature (13)
May I . . . ? (1)
May I bring you . . . ? (2)
Maybe . . . can (5)
Maybe . . . could (5)
Maybe . . . should (5)
Maybe so. (6)
medium rare (7)
Michigan (6)
midnight (2)
might (6)
mild (5)
miles (3)
mind (3)
miss (3)
models (10)
Morning. (3)
mortgage (10)
motto (13)
must [obviously] (3)
My name is . . . (1)
My pleasure. (1)

N

neat (3)
nephew (13)
nervous (2)
net (5)
New Jersey (12)
Nice to meet you. (2)
no longer in service (7)
No problem. (4)
No sweat. (4)
No way! (5)
nonstop (4)
Nope. (4)
Not a chance! (5)
Nothing much. (5)

O

occasionally (2)
o'clock (1)
off [on one's way] (7)
Oh my! (13)
on (my) way over (4)
on-the-job training (12)
or else (7)
ought to (10)
ounces (13)
over [to that place] (7)
over [more than] (11)
owe (12)

P

pal (7)
paper (9)
paperwork (5)
parades (6)
parking (2)
pasta (1)
patient [adj] (6)
patients [n] (5)
paw (7)
pediatrician (1)
peephole (2)
permanently (3)
pet (7)
photo album (1)
photographer (1)
Pick up the pace. (4)
picked out (10)
picking (him) up (3)
pictures (1)
pitcher (10)
Pleasant dreams. (3)
Please forgive me. (2)
Pleased to meet you. (2)
point (1)
pony (4)

pooch (7)
Pop (5)
pounds (13)
pour (6)
practically (12)
pregnant (11)
production staff (10)
program (5)
promised (8)
property (11)
protein (6)
pumpkin pie (6)
purchase (11)
purse (3)
put money down (11)
put (it) off (8)
put (my experience) on the line (12)
put (my mind) to good use (12)
put up (11)

Q
quite a (+ n) (5)

R
railroad (3)
ranch (11)
raw (7)
read (this) over (11)
real (12)
real-estate agent (11)
real-estate section (11)
reassurance (8)
reception room (10)
recipe (6)
redesigning (12)
references (7)
refinancing (11)
refrigerator (5)
remove (8)
replaces (13)
reschedule (8)
researched (3)
resemble (13)
reservation [arrangement to hold a table in a restaurant] (2)
reservations [feelings of not being sure] (9)
residence (7)
resolve (12)
restless (12)
résumé (12)
retired (3)

Right. [to agree to do something] (10)
roads (3)
room (11)
runs (12)

S
salaries (11)
savings (11)
scared (9)
scary (9)
schedule (5)
scheduling (8)
schools (9)
scissors (4)
scoop (1)
see [understand] (6)
see to (it) (8)
sensitive (13)
set (4)
set up (3)
settlers (6)
Shall we. . . ? (2)
sheets (11)
shelter (7)
shipped (3)
shopping malls (12)
shy (10)
silly (7)
sister-in-law (2)
site (12)
sketches (10)
slam (the door) (6)
Small world. (3)
Smell the flowers. (10)
Snow White and the Seven Dwarfs (8)
so (+ adj) (7)
So (do I). (13)
So long. (5)
some [a wonderful] (12)
something [great] (3)
son (5)
sore loser (8)
sore throats (8)
spaceship (10)
speaking of (2)
spoil (5)
starving (2)
stocks (11)
stomachache (2)
street vendor (2)
stubborn (11)
stuff (1)
such a (+ adj + n) (7)

sunny (5)
Sure can. (12)
switch (4)

T
take a (little) break (6)
take after (13)
Take care. (11)
take care of (everything) (2)
Take it easy. (1)
take time off (3)
Take your time. (3)
talk business (12)
talk (this) over (8)
tango (4)
tax forms (11)
tea kettle (3)
teases (4)
teddy bears (13)
Thanks. (1)
Thanks, anyway. (1)
That's for sure. (3)
That's it. [That's the end.] (4)
That's it. [You're doing well.] (5)
That's music to my ears. (12)
the best (9)
the Big Apple (3)
the Bronx (1)
The price is right. (11)
the simple things in life (10)
the toughest (9)
The traffic is very heavy. (1)
the worst (9)
theater reviews (9)
There you go. (10)
thirty [time] (1)
This is . . . [to introduce someone] (1)
This is he. [for answering the telephone] (7)
thoughtful (7)
thrilled (5)
till (3)
time on (my) hands (12)
Times (11)
TLC (13)
to be exact (3)
to carry on (the Stewart name) (13)
to have (me) around (12)
tonsillectomies (8)
too (3)

touchdown (6)
towels (13)
toy (1)
tradition (11)
traffic (2)
traffic light (2)
train (11)
transcript (9)
trunk (3)
try (it) on (1)
tuition (9)
tummy (2)
turkey dressing (6)
turn (it) in (9)
turns out (9)
twin (10)

U
Uh-oh. (5)
umbrella stand (2)
unfortunately (7)
uptown platform (1)
used to (10)

V
valuable (12)
vice-president (2)

W
walnuts (6)
washcloth (13)
weight (13)
Welcome aboard! (12)
well done (5)
well trained (7)
What (+ adj + n)! (2)
What about . . . ? (1)
What do you do for a living? (4)
What do you mean? (4)
What do you say we . . . (5)
What does (your father) do? (1)
What for? (10)
What'll it be? (10)
What's gotten into (him)? (6)
What's the matter? (2)
What's the weather going be like? (5)
What's up? (7)
Where did the time go? (
Why [to show surprise] (3
Why don't we . . . ? (5)

will be (+ -*ing* verb) (3)
will do   [is enough] (7)
Will do. [I'll do it.] (10)
wise (9)
with my own two hands
   (12)
without a doubt (4)
wondering (3)
work at (it) (5)

working on (9)
work out (v) (4)
work (something) out (8)
would [used to] (10)
Would you kindly . . . ? (3)
Would you like . . . ? (2)
Wow! (6)
wrap (5)
Wrong number. (6)

X

Y
Yeah. (2)
Yes, indeed. (3)
you [impersonal pronoun]
   (13)
You bet! (5)
You can count on it. (13)

You name the day.
   (3)
You really saved the day
   (for me). (1)
You're welcome. (1)
Yup. (6)

Z